First published in 2009 by

Appletree Press Ltd
The Old Potato Station
14 Howard Street South
Belfast BT7 1AP

Tel: +44 (0) 28 90 243 074
Fax: +44 (0) 28 90 246 756
Web Site: www.appletree.ie
E-mail: reception@appletree.ie

First published in 2000 as *The Irish Quiz Book*

A catalogue record for this book
is available from the British Library.

The Great Irish Quiz Book

ISBN 978-1-84758-128-0

9 8 7 6 5 4 3 2 1

AP3611

THE GREAT
IRISH QUIZ BOOK

JIM BLACK

Appletree Press

1. The Ox Mountains in Mayo are also known as?

2. Where is Ireland's tallest round tower?

3. Shannon Airport is situated between which rivers?

4. Where is 'the lake isle of Innisfree'?

5. Name the lighthouse above Whitehead on the Antrim coast.

6. Which lough lies below Lough Conn?

7. Which lough lies between Loughs Corra and Corrib?

8. How many columns make up the Giant's Causeway?

9. Which rock makes up each of the columns in the Causeway?

10. How many counties are there in Northern Ireland?

11. How many counties are there in the Republic of Ireland?

12. What is the most northerly county in Ireland?

13. What is the main catch in Lough Neagh?

14. Which famous river runs through Dublin?

15. Which new counties were created in 1608?

16. Where was the ancient 'Tara' brooch found?

17. Around which ancient site did Daniel O'Connell organise his first large rally?

18. Which county of the Pale was once called 'Queen's County'?

19. What is Ireland's largest offshore island?

20. Where is Ossian buried?

Answers to Quiz 01

1. Slieve Gamph

2. Limerick

3. Fergus and Shannon

4. On Lough Gill in Co. Sligo

5. Black Head

6. Lough Corrib

7. Lough Mask

8. 40,000

9. Basalt

10. Six

11. Twenty-six

12. Donegal

13. Eels

14. The Liffey

15. Armagh, Cavan, Coleraine, Donegal, Fermanagh, Tyrone

16. On a beach at Bettystown, Drogheda

17. Tara, Co. Meath

18. Leix (now Laois)

19. Achill Island

20. Ossian's Grave, on Tievebulliagh, near Cushendall in Co. Antrim

1. Which pretender to the English throne was crowned in Dublin?

2. Who founded the settlement which became Dublin?

3. What was the Inauguration Stone of the Irish kings?

4. Where was Sir Arthur Wellesley, later British Prime Minister, born?

5. During which years did the notorious Irish Potato Famine take place?

6. According to the Julian calendar, what was the date of the Battle of the Boyne?

7. Which rebellion is remembered by Slaughterford Bridge on Islandmagee and Bloody Bridge near Newcastle in Co. Down?

8. Which north Antrim coastal ruin was once the home of the O'Cathain clan?

9. Who led the United Irishmen in rebellion in 1798 in Antrim, only to be hanged in Cornmarket in Belfast?

10. In which organisation was Wolfe Tone prominent?

11. Thurgesius was king of which people?

12. When was the border of Northern Ireland and the Republic of Ireland agreed?

13. Which system of justice had been considered as an alternative to British law in Ireland during 1919-21?

14. Who was elected MP for North Tipperary in 1875, only to lose his seat as he was an escaped convict?

15. Which of Queen Elizabeth I's favourites once owned Lismore Castle, Co. Waterford?

16. When was the first recorded Irish parliament?

17. In which sport was Jack Lynch an outstanding player before entering political life?

18. Which Irish nationalist published *The Re-conquest of Ireland* in 1915?

19. Which state office did WB Yeats hold in 1922?

20. Who founded the Society of the United Irishmen?

1. Lambert Simnel, 1487

2. Thurgesius

3. Lia fail (the Stone of Destiny, which was transported to Scotland)

4. Merrion Street, Dublin

5. 1845-49

6. 1st July 1690

7. The 1641 Catholic Rebellion

8. Dunseverick Castle

9. Henry Joy McCracken

10. The United Irishmen

11. Norsemen, Vikings

12. 1925, between the governments of Northern Ireland, Eire, Great Britain

13. Brehon law

14. John Mitchel

15. Sir Walter Raleigh

16. 1264

17. Hurling

18. James Connolly

19. Irish senator

20. Theobald Wolfe Tone

1. Snooker World Champion Dennis Taylor is from which town in Co. Tyrone?

2. Which sport do Finn Harps play?

3. Which Irish sport is sometimes confused with the Scottish game shinty?

4. Mary Peters won Olympic Gold in which athletics event in 1972?

5. State the final score in 1887's first proper Hurling Final under GAA rules.

6. What was the original title of the GAA, the Gaelic Athletic Association?

7. Which Irish horse racing trainer won the Irish 1000 Guineas, Irish 2000 Guineas, Irish St Leger, Irish Derby, King George VI and Queen Elizabeth stakes in 1963?

8. Which sport was involved in, but absent from, the formation of the GAA?

9. Where was the formation meeting of the GAA held?

10. In which team sport did Ireland win Silver in 1908 Olympics?

11. What is Limerick's main rugby venue?

12. Name the counties represented at the formation of the Ladies Gaelic Football Association?

13. What is forbidden in Ladies' Football?

14. Where was Ireland's first Rugby Football Club established?

15. Ireland's first rugby international against England in 1875 fielded how many players to a side?

16. Which Irish boxing champion instructed Daniel Day-Lewis in his film portrayal of *The Boxer*?

17. Where was the world's first 'steeplechase' run?

18. Why was the 'steeplechase' so termed?

19. After whom is the Higher Education hurling cup, The Fitzgibbon Cup, named?

20. Which organisation is titled 'Cumann Peile Gael na mBan'?

1. Coalisland

2. Football (soccer)

3. Hurling

4. Pentathlon

5. Tipperary beat Galway by one goal and one point to no score (1-1 to 0-0)

6. The Gaelic Athletic Association for the Preservation and Cultivation of our national Pastimes

7. PJ Prendergast

8. Billiards

9. The billiard-room of Miss Hayes's Commercial Hotel in Thurles

10. Hockey

11. Thomond Park

12. Galway, Kerry, Offaly and Tipperary

13. Deliberate bodily contact

14. Dublin University, in 1854

15. Twenty

16. Barry McGuigan

17. Mallow, Co. Cork, 1752

18. Horses raced between two church spires (steeples)

19. Dr Edwin Fitzgibbon, priest, Philosophy Professor, University College, Cork (1911-36)

20. Ladies Gaelic Football Association

1. Who was leader of Clan na Poblachta?

2. What was the title of the Irish Volunteers' newspaper?

3. When did the first woman win a seat in the House of Commons?

4. When did the first woman to be elected to the British Parliament take her seat?

5. When was President Douglas Hyde born?

6. The Irish flag is similar in design (but in the opposite order) to that of which African nation?

7. Which politician said "I found Ireland on her knees…Ireland is now a nation"?

8. Where was the birth-place of the man who became Irish President on 17th June 1959?

9. What is the role of the Ceann Comhairle in Irish politics?

10. Which Irishman became Austrian governor of Dalmatia?

11. Kitty O'Shea's husband was once MP for which Irish constituency?

12. Who first used the phrase 'Ulster will fight: Ulster will be right'?

13. When was Clan na Poblachta formed?

14. When was Erskine Childers elected President of Ireland?

15. When did Erskine Childers, President of Ireland die?

16. When was Sinn Féin formed?

17. When was Cumann na nGaedhael formed?

18. When did Cumann na nGaedhael cease to exist? Why?

19. Which post did John Costello hold after de Valera (Twice)?

20. Who was the first leader of the DUP?

Answers to Quiz 04

1. Sean MacBride

2. *An tÓglach*

3. Constance Markiewicz, 28th December 1918

4. Constance Markiewicz declined to sit in the British Parliament

5. 17th January 1860

6. Ivory Coast (Côte d'Ivoire)

7. Henry Grattan

8. New York

9. The Speaker of the Irish Parliament

10. Thomas Brady, 1752-1857

11. Clare

12. Lord Randolph Churchill, in 1886

13. 6th July 1946

14. 30th May 1973

15. 7th November 1974

16. 1905

17. 1923

18. 1933. It changed its name.

19. He was Taoiseach after de Valera in 1948, and de Valera regained the office in 1951. Costello took office again in 1954.

20. Rev. Ian Paisley

1. Name the writer of the book on which the film *The Commitments* was based?

2. What is the name of Frank McCourt's follow-up memoir to *Angela's Ashes*?

3. What was the title of Bram Stoker's first novel?

4. Which Roddy Doyle novel won the Booker Prize in 1993?

5. When was James Joyce born?

6. When was *Ulysses* first published?

7. Which philosopher, born in Dublin, published *Philosophical Inquiry into the Origin of our Ideas of the Sublime and Beautiful* in 1756?

8. Which work by James Joyce became the novel, *A Portrait of the Artist as a Young Man*?

9. Which Irish poet's works include *The Poetry of WB Yeats*?

10. Why is the *Book of the Dun Cow* so-called?

11. Scrapings from early Irish books were said by the historian Bede to be effective against which threat to life?

12. What was CS Lewis' full name?

13. Who is the main character in *The Cattle Raid of Cooley*?

14. What does the *Book of Kells* contain?

15. Which Bernard McLaverty book was made into a film starring Liam Neeson as a priest?

16. What is the oldest surviving manuscript written completely in the Irish language?

17. How many books did St Colmcille write in his own hand?

18. Which Irish royal acropolis was used as the name of Scarlett O'Hara's home?

19. Who wrote *Leabhar Gabhalla* or the *Book of Invasions*?

20. The *Book of Invasions* describes the history of Ireland from which date?

1. Roddy Doyle

2. *'Tis*

3. *The Primrose Path*

4. *Paddy Clarke Ha Ha Ha*

5. 2nd February 1882

6. 2nd February 1922

7. Edmund Burke

8. *Stephen Hero*

9. Louis MacNeice

10. From the colour of the hide of the animal on which the text was written

11. Snake venom (possibly because of the link to St Patrick)

12. Clive Staples Lewis

13. Cuchulainn

14. The Gospels

15. *Lamb*

16. *The Book of the Dun Cow*

17. 300, according to annals of Clonmacnois

18. Tara

19. Micheál Ó Cléirigh

20. From the beginning of Time – it features the Biblical story of Creation as well as a history of Ireland.

1. What was the Tain Bo Cualigne?

2. Who or what was the ard-rí?

3. What is 'Luan'?

4. Which month in Irish is Bealtaine?

5. What is 'rugby' in Irish?

6. What does 'fada' mean in English?

7. What does 'fainne' mean in English?

8. What does a 'fada' do to a vowel?

9. What is the Oireachtas?

10. What was an 'ollamh'?

11. Which animal is called 'grainneog' in Irish?

12. What is a 'neamhóg'?

13. What is 'Chumann Sléibhteoireachta na hÉireann'?

14. What does the name 'Dougal' mean in Irish?

15. What is 'uisce beatha'?

16. What is a 'clochán'?

17. What is 'An Chomhairle Ealaíon'?

18. What is 'Céadaoin'?

19. What is 'Déardaoin'?

20. What does 'Feabhra' mean?

Answers to Quiz 06

1. The Cattle Raid of Cooley

2. High King of Ireland

3. Monday

4. May

5. Rugbaí

6. Long

7. Ring

8. It stresses and stretches the sound

9. Irish Parliament

10. A poet, an historian

11. The hedgehog

12. An animal-skin boat from Co. Kerry

13. Irish Mountaineering Club

14. Dark stranger: 'dubh' black, 'gall' stranger

15. Irish whiskey

16. A 'beehive' stone structure

17. The Arts Council of Ireland

18. Wednesday

19. Thursday

20. February

1. What is the real name of the lead singer in *The Commitments*?

2. Which road did The Saw Doctors sing about in a song of home-sickness and emigration?

3. Which instrument is James Galway world-famous for playing?

4. What was unusual about James Galway's most famous instrument?

5. Bob Geldof co-wrote the song 'Do They Know It's Christmas' with which other singer?

6. When did Bob Geldof's fund-raising Live Aid concert take place?

7. George Friedrich Handel was said to have used the organ in which church while composing his *Messiah*?

8. In which town was the 'Londonderry Air' first noted down?

9. What is the song the 'Londonderry Air' better known as?

10. HF Lyte, curate of Taghmon, Co. Wexford, 1815, wrote which hymn?

11. John McCormack, Irish singer, was famous for which singing voice?

12. *Paddy on the Road* was the 1969 debut album of which Irish singer-songwriter?

13. Which musical form was taken as the title of a famous Irish folk group?

14. Which Irish musician was once part of folk group Steeleye Span and The Pogues?

15. Who wrote the theme music for the television series *Father Ted*?

16. What is Van Morrison's full name?

17. In what year were The Pogues formed?

18. Sean O'Farrell is featured in which 19th-century ballad?

19. What is the title of Ash's debut album?

20. Which Thin Lizzy album shares its title with a Roman Polanski film?

1. Andrew Strong

2. The N17

3. The flute

4. It was made of gold

5. Midge Ure

6. 13th July 1985

7. St Michan's, Dublin

8. Limavady, Co. Derry

9. Danny Boy

10. 'Abide with Me'

11. Tenor

12. Christy Moore

13. Planxty

14. Terry Woods

15. Neil Hannon

16. George Ivan Morrison

17. 1982

18. 'The Rising of the Moon'

19. *1977*

20. *Chinatown*

1. Who wrote, of whom? 'fanatic, bad actress, figure of fun – She was called each.'

2. What 'geographical' term was used to describe the 19th-century Irish gentry?

3. Which grandson of an Irish immigrant made the most famous Irish film? Name the film.

4. Who was the most famous resident of Derrynane House in Co. Kerry?

5. Which Irish resident developed the pneumatic tyre?

6. Why was James Ussher famous?

7. By which noble title was William Parsons known?

8. What is Inis mac Nesain?

9. Who called himself 'Duke of Ireland'?

10. Which famous sailor began an extensive survey of Dublin waters in December 1800?

11. Where was 'the Irish rebel' James Connolly born?

12. What does the name 'Ossian' mean?

13. What does O'Riordan mean in Irish?

14. Who founded the Presentation Order?

15. What office did John Brinkley hold on his retirement in 1826?

16. Which Irish figurehead wrote 'Romantic Ireland's dead and gone / It's with O'Leary in the grave'?

17. Who said "English is the native language of Irishmen"?

18. The scientist John Joly pioneered which art form?

19. Who attacked the Co. Cork fishing town of Baltimore in the 17th century, carrying away people to slavery in Africa?

20. Which cleric-poet was once Professor of Greek at University College Dublin?

1. C Day-Lewis, of Constance Markiewicz

2. West Britons

3. John Ford, *The Quiet Man*

4. Daniel O'Connell

5. John Boyd Dunlop

6. He calculated the date of Creation, from Biblical information

7. 3rd Earl of Rosse

8. Ireland's Eye

9. Thomas Stucley, 16th-century adventurer

10. Captain Bligh, notorious captain of the *Bounty*

11. Edinburgh, Scotland

12. 'little fawn', from the Celtic

13. Royal poet ('riogh' royal, 'bardán', poet, bard)

14. Miss Nano Nagle

15. Bishop of Cloyne

16. WB Yeats

17. George Bernard Shaw

18. A system of colour photography

19. Pirates from Algiers, led by a man from Dungarvan

20. Gerard Manley Hopkins

1. George Bernard Shaw was awarded the Nobel Prize for Literature. How was his work described in the Nobel citation?

2. Giorgio and Lucia were the first-born of which Irish writer?

3. Who was the mother of Giorgio and Lucia, children of an Irish writer?

4. Who landed at Derry on 20th May 1932, the first woman to fly across the Atlantic?

5. Charles Stewart Parnell was named as co-respondent in the divorce of which couple?

6. Which Dublin-born British admiral received the surrender of the Italian fleet in September 1943?

7. What was Henry Joy McCracken's original calling?

8. Who founded the newspaper *The United Irishman*?

9. What was the first name of the revolutionary O'Donovan Rossa?

10. Who was the first person to be charged under the Treason-Felony Act of 1848?

11. What is the real name of the 'Colleen Bawn'?

12. What was Lady Wilde also known as?

14. Who was the 'fair-haired wonder from Cahirciveen'?

15. What is Maureen Fitzsimons famous for?

16. Which Irish writer became business manager to the actor, Henry Irving?

17. Which Irish poet was a BBC producer and playwright throughout World War II?

18. How many sons did Niall of the Nine Hostages have?

19. Poet C Day-Lewis was father to which now-Irish actor?

20. By what name is Maelmadoc Ua Morgair better known?

1. GB Shaw's work was described as being "marked by both idealism and humanity."

2. James Joyce

3. Nora Barnacle

4. Amelia Earhart

5. William Henry O'Shea and Katherine (Kitty) O'Shea

6. Andrew Browne Cunningham, 1st Viscount Cunningham of Hyndhope

7. He was a Belfast linen manufacturer

8. John Mitchel

9. Jeremiah

10. John Mitchel

11. Ellen Hanley

12. Speranza

14. Jerome O'Shea, Kerry goalie of the 1950s

15. As the real name of Maureen O'Hara

16. Bram Stoker

17. Louis MacNeice

18. Fourteen

19. Daniel Day-Lewis: born in England, he is now an Irish citizen

20. St Malachy, bishop of Armagh

1. In which northern county was Nobel Poetry Laureate Seamus Heaney born?

2. Which Irish poet was awarded the Nobel Prize in 1923?

3. The Aeir, or Satire of the Bards, was capable of what feat?

4. When did WB Yeats die?

5. Who wrote the poem 'The Lark in the Clear Air'?

6. Who wrote 'The Croppy Boy'?

7. Who wrote the poem 'The Famine Year'?

8. Who wrote 'We are wretches, famished, scorned, human tools to build
    your pride'?

9. Who wrote the poem 'I am Ireland'?

10. Which Irish poet died in Flanders on 31st July 1917?

11. Which poet wrote the first manifesto of the United Irishmen?

12. What were Oliver Goldsmith's last words, in reply to the enquiry
    'Is your mind at ease?'

13. Which poet wrote 'Ireland is hooey'?

14. Which poet wrote 'Stella's Birthday, 1720'?

15. Who was the subject of Eileen O'Leary's poem entitled 'The Lament for…'?

16. Which poet wrote 'An Irish Airman Foresees His Death'?

17. In which poem does William McBurney declare the following?
    'I bear no hate against living thing / But I love my country above my king'

18. Who wrote the following? 'They'll say I came in Eighteen-seventy-one
    And died in Dublin…'

19. Name the person of whom Francis Ledwidge wrote 'He shall not hear the
    bittern cry / In the wild sky, where he is lain'.

20. The character of Buck Mulligan in *Ulysses* is based on which poet?

Answers to Quiz 10

1. Derry

2. WB Yeats

3. Physical harm against the listener it was aimed at

4. 28th January 1939

5. Samuel Ferguson

6. William McBurney

7. Lady Wilde

8. Lady Wilde, 'The Famine Year'

9. Padraig Pearse

10. Francis Ledwidge

11. William Drennan

12. "No, it is not"

13. Louis MacNeice

14. Jonathan Swift

15. Art O'Leary

16. WB Yeats

17. 'The Croppy Boy'

18. JM Synge

19. Thomas McDonough

20. Oliver St John Gogarty

1. Kissing the Stone in Blarney Castle is thought by many to confer which useful talent?

2. What are the Stags of Broad Haven?

3. What is The Rower?

4. Rathlin island has how many lighthouses?

5. Name the author of this question: 'Am I a free man in England, and do I become a slave in six hours by crossing the Channel?'

6. Which Irish province sounds like a German state?

7. Why did James Joyce not protest against Japan's attack on Pearl Harbor, 7th December 1941?

8. What was a 'gallowglass'?

9. What were 'crannogs'?

10. A statue in the GPO commemorating the 1916 Rising takes as its model which mythical figure?

11. What was Ireland's first University?

12. What were 'Hedge Schools' in the 18th century?

13. Daniel O'Connell was buried in Glasnevin cemetery in Dublin, without which organ?

14. What is a 'donnybrook'?

15. What is the origin of 'donnybrook'?

16. What sort of animals race at Shelbourne Park Race Track?

17. Which Irish county gave its name to a famous Zorro?

18. On what date each year is 'Bloomsday' celebrated?

19. Why were defeated chiefs sometimes blinded?

20. What was 'The Pale'?

Answers to Quiz 11

1. The gift of the gab

2. Islands off the coast of Mayo

3. A town or townland near New Ross

4. Three

5. Jonathan Swift

6. Munster

7. Because he died on 13th January 1941

8. A Scottish soldier who fought in Ireland; 'foreign warrior' in Irish is 'gall óglach'

9. Man-made islands on which wooden fortifications were built

10. Cuchulainn

11. Trinity College, Dublin, founded 1592

12. Formal education for Catholics was prevented by Penal Laws: children were taught in fields at any opportunity

13. His heart, which was left in the Church of St Agatha in Rome

14. A riotous assembly, an all-in fight

15. A fair held in Donnybrook, Dublin

16. Greyhounds

17. Tyrone (as in Tyrone Power)

18. 16th June

19. A disfigured person was considered ineligible for election as king or chief

20. An area around Dublin, into Leinster

1. Where did Leopold Bloom, of *Ulysses* fame, live?

2. What was the full name of Joyce Carey, novelist?

3. What was the title of Samuel Beckett's first novel?

4. Who wrote the collection of short stories entitled *The Ballroom of Romance*?

5. Who wrote *At Swim-Two-Birds*?

6. When was author William Trevor Cox born?

7. Who wrote *Some Experiences of an Irish RM*?

8. What was Irish 19th-century author Ross' first name?

9. Who wrote *The Life Story of Éamon de Valera*?

10. For which novel was Iris Murdoch awarded the Booker Prize?

11. From which myth cycle was *The Cattle Raid of Cooley* taken?

12. In what language was the *Book of Kells* written?

13. Who wrote *The Quare Fellow*?

14. Sheridan le Fanu's *Carmilla* is a variation on which legendary monster?

15. In which year is the book *Ulysses* set?

16. 'Father Prout' was the pen-name of which writer and one-time priest?

17. John O'Leary, Fenian, is immortalised by Yeats in which poem?

18. Which poet is reputed to have written part of his *Faerie Queen* at Lismore Castle?

19. In which language did Brian Merriman write 'The Midnight Court'?

20. Against whom would Irish monks recite 'A furore Normanorum libera nos, Domine'?

1. No. 7, Eccles Street, Dublin

2. Arthur Joyce Lunel Carey

3. *Murphy*

4. William Trevor

5. Flann O'Brien

6. 24th May 1928

7. Somerville and Ross

8. Martin

9. Sean O'Faolain

10. *The Sea, The Sea*

11. The Red Branch Cycle

12. Latin

13. Brendan Behan

14. Vampires

15. 1904

16. Francis Sylvester O'Mahony

17. 'September 1913'

18. Edmund Spenser

19. Irish

10. The Vikings – 'From the fury of the Norsemen Lord deliver us'

1. What is the origin of the name Tallaght, Co. Dublin?

2. Which rock is said in folklore to be the result of demonic indigestion?

3. What is the county town of Roscommon?

4. What is the county town of Monaghan?

5. What is the county town of Sligo?

6. Which counties in the Province of Ulster are not part of Northern Ireland?

7. Where is the geographical centre of Ireland?

8. What is Ireland's second smallest county?

9. Where would you find the Jealous Wall?

10. In which county is Blarney Castle?

11. From where did the 'Flight of the Earls' take place?

12. Bunclody in Co. Wicklow has another name. What is it?

13. What is Ireland's smallest county?

14. Where is the National Maritime Museum?

15. Complete the title of this Oliver Goldsmith work – *Citizen of...*?

16. What was the capital of the ancient Province of South Leinster?

17. Which county did Coleraine become?

18. Where did the Ulster Canal originate?

19. Where do the rivers Barrow and Nore rise?

20. What are Ireland's three highest mountains?

1. Maelruan's Plague Grave
2. Rock of Cashel – the Devil took a bite from a mountain, but then spat it into the sea
3. Roscommon
4. Monaghan
5. Sligo
6. Cavan, Donegal and Monaghan
7. Birr, Co. Offaly
8. Carlow
9. Belvedere, Co. Westmeath
10. Co. Cork
11. Rathmullan, Lough Swilly, Co. Donegal
12. Newtownbarry
13. Louth
14. Dun Laoghaire
15. *The World*
16. Dinn Rig, on the river Barrow
17. Londonderry / Derry
18. Belturbet, Co. Cavan
19. In the Slieve Bloom range
20. Carrantuohill, Beenkeragh and Caher (3414, 3314, 3200 feet)

1. The quarry of Starch Hill was used as the source of stone for the construction of which Irish castle?

2. In 841AD, which two Irish ports were seized by Vikings?

3. In what year were the first Viking raids on the Irish coast?

4. Brehon law operated mainly by the use of which punishment?

5. When was Brian Boru born?

6. What is the origin of the title 'Boru'?

7. Who became King of Munster in 976AD?

8. When did Brian Boru become the first High King of Ireland?

9. Which battle did Brian Boru win in 1014?

10. In which battle did Brian Boru die?

11. Which city was stormed by Strongbow before his marriage to Aoife?

12. In what year did the Plantation of Ulster begin, with publication of *The Articles of Plantation*?

13. Which battle took place on 12th July 1691?

14. What is the Irish connection of the sole US Army survivor of Little Big Horn?

15. Who was known as the 'Father of the American Navy'?

16. Sir Arthur Wellesley, soldier and statesman, was also known as?

17. When did the 'Flight of the Earls' take place?

18. Pope Alexander III gave Henry II which title?

19. When did Oliver Cromwell land in Ireland?

20. When were Derry's gates most famously closed?

1. Blarney Castle

2. Dublin and Anagassan (between Dundalk and Drogheda)

3. 807AD

4. Fines

5. *c.* 840AD

6. From Borinne, near Killaloe, Co Clare

7. Brian Boru

8. 1002

9. Clontarf

10. Clontarf, 1014

11. Waterford

12. 1607

13. Aughrim

14. Commanche, horse of Myles Keogh, Irish soldier who fought with Custer

15. John Barry

16. The Duke of Wellington

17. 14th September 1607

18. Lord of Ireland

19. 15th August 1649

20. 7th December 1688

1. What does 'Iúil' mean?

2. Which month in Irish is 'mí na Samhain'?

3. What does the 'fainne' signify today?

4. What does 'glas' mean in Irish?

5. What would you do with 'brachán caoireola'?

6. What is 'colcannon'?

7. What is 'spideog' in English?

8. What is Ceannanus Mór in Co. Antrim?

9. What is 'Bord na Gaeilge'?

10. What is the meaning of Irish word 'Corr'?

11. What is 'Mhairt'?

12. What is 'Aoine'?

13. What does 'Éanair' mean?

14. What does 'Márta' mean?

15. The Irish language symbol of a left to right diagonal is called?

16. What is gaelic football in Irish?

17. What is a 'sliotar'?

18. What does TD stand for?

19. What is Dáil Éireann?

20. What was a 'seanachie'?

Answers to Quiz 15

1. July
2. November
3. It is a pin which shows the wearer's ease in Irish
4. Green
5. Eat it – it's a mutton broth
6. A potato and cabbage dish
7. The robin
8. Kells
9. Irish Language Board, promoting the use of the Irish language
10. Heron
11. Tuesday
12. Friday
13. January
14. March
15. Fada
16. Peile Gaelach
17. A hurling ball
18. Teachta Dála, member of Irish parliament
19. Irish House of Representatives
20. A storyteller or bard

1. Where were the group Clannad formed?

2. Clannad won a Grammy Award in which category for their album *Landmarks*?

3. Where was the writer of 'international anthem' 'The Red Flag' born?

4. Dolores O'Riordan was famously lead singer of which band?

5. Lord Mountcharles is connected with which high-profile Irish musical festival?

6. What is Dana's real name?

7. Who composed the music to the stage show, Riverdance?

8. Which Irish singer was called 'the Empress of Ireland' by Toscanini?

9. Who wrote the words to 'A Soldier's Song'?

10. Which style of music was Rory Gallagher famous for?

11. Which two instruments does Van Morrison usually play?

12. Which Irish radio DJ is famous for his 'Fab 50'?

13. For which charity organisation was 'Feed the World' the theme song?

14. What is the full 'title' of Bono, from U2?

15. What is the origin of Bono's 'title'?

16. In the song, exactly how many 'shades of green' can be found in Ireland?

17. Who composed the melody which went on to be used in the music to the 'Star-Spangled Banner'?

18. The Pogues and Kirsty MacColl sang of 'Fairytale of…'?

19. What is the origin of the band title 'The Pogues'?

20. Who was lead singer of The Pogues in the 1980s?

Answers to Quiz 16

1. Leo's Tavern, Gweedore, Donegal

2. New Age

3. Co. Meath, 1850

4. The Cranberries

5. Slane

6. Rosemary Brown

7. Bill Whelan

8. Margaret Burke Sheridan

9. Peadar Kearney, 1883-1942

10. Guitar-based blues

11. Guitar and harmonica

12. Dave Fanning

13. Band Aid / Live Aid

14. Bono Vox

15. From a sign advertising a hearing aid – 'Bono Vox'

16. Forty

17. Turlough O'Carolan

18. 'New York'

19. 'Póg mo' means 'kiss my' in Irish, 'hoan' refers to the posterior

20. Shane MacGowan

1. Which Irish saint argued that Pope Gregory's calendar was mistaken?

2. The dating of which religious festival was subject to disagreement between an Irish saint and the Gregorian calendar?

3. Who said "righteousness without culture has a tendency to turn rancid"?

4. As what did James Larkin find notoriety?

5. Dublin's Pro-Cathedral is also known as?

6. Who conducted the *Messiah* on its first performance?

7. Who was known as Silken Thomas?

8. Which 18th-century Franciscan prior became known as the 'apostle of Newfoundland'?

9. Irish President Mary McAleese was a Professor in which University prior to her election?

10. After whom is the establishment in *question 9* named?

11. Where was Irish dancing superstar Michael Flatley born?

12. What was the name of the chieftain who brought St Patrick to Slemish?

13. Who was the first and last Lord Esmonde?

14. Daniel O'Connell once refused to take an oath: his famous reason?

15. What was the origin of Wexford's Bargy dialect?

16. What is Olympic swimmer Michelle Smith's married name?

17. When was Edmund Burke born?

18. Who founded the Order, Sisters of Mercy?

19. To which Irish saint was a holy well near Liscannor, Co. Clare, dedicated?

20. Who was the Marquis de St Ruth?

1. Columbanus

2. Easter

3. Arland Ussher, 1949

4. A leader of workers' strikes and Union organisation

5. Cathedral of St Mary's (Roman Catholic)

6. George Freidrich Handel, the composer

7. Lord Thomas FitzGerald, in the 16th century

8. James Louis O'Donnell

9. Queen's University Belfast

10. Queen Victoria

11. United States of America

12. Milchu

13. Laurence – his descendants were Baronets

14. "part of it I know to be false, another part I believe not to be true"

15. Norman settlers of Welsh and Flemish origin

16. Michelle de Bruin

17. 1st January 1730

18. Catherine McAuley

19. St Brigid

20. A French general on the side of King James, 1691

1. Who said after being sentenced to death, "When my country takes her place among the nations of the earth, then and not until then, let my epitaph be written"?

2. Who said "no political change whatsoever is worth the shedding of a single drop of human blood"?

3. Who challenged Daniel O'Connell to a duel in 1815?

4. Who said "Ireland unfree shall never be at peace"?

5. How many children did Kitty O'Shea bear Charles Stewart Parnell?

6. To whom was Scrabo Tower, Newtownards, Co. Down, dedicated?

7. Who was brought to the aptly named Abbey of Swords in 1014?

8. Which Irish Antarctic explorer found the remains of Robert Falcon Scott's fatal expedition in 1911?

9. Who founded an Irish Scout movement in August 1909?

10. Who is credited with coining the phrase which became GUBU?

11. Which Irish-born author died the same day as President Kennedy and Aldous Huxley?

12. What was 'Napper' Tandy's first name?

13. Which famous musician was born in Nobber, Co. Meath, in 1670?

14. What great age was Catherine, second wife of 12th Earl of Desmond reputed to have reached?

15. Where was Tom Crean born?

16. Which Irishman was the first European to sight Antarctica, 1819?

17. WHD Boyle, related to scientist Robert Boyle, held which military post?

18. James Charles O'Connor from Cork was noted for promoting which language?

19. What was Cuchulainn's original name?

20. Which Irish physicist was awarded the Nobel Prize in 1951?

Answers to Quiz 18

1. Robert Emmet

2. Daniel O'Connell

3. Sir Robert Peel, Chief Secretary to Ireland

4. Padraig Pearse

5. Three

6. 3rd Marquis of Londonderry, 1851

7. The deceased king Brian Boru and his dead son Murrough, after the Battle of Clontarf

8. Tom Crean

9. Constance Markiewicz

10. Charles Haughey, 13th August 1982

11. CS Lewis

12. James

13. Turlough O'Carolan

14. Accounts vary between 110 and 162 years of age

15. Annascaul, Co. Kerry

16. Edward Bansfield, born in Cork in 1783

17. Admiral of the Fleet (Royal Navy)

18. Esperanto

19. Setanta

20. Ernest Thomas Sinton Walton

1. Which of C Day-Lewis' ancestors was also a poet of renown?

2. In which poem did Samuel Beckett write 'I would like my love to die'?

3. Which poet described Belfast as 'Built on reclaimed mud'?

4. Which poem opens as follows: 'Sweet was the sound / When oft at evening's close'?

5. In which language did Jonathan Swift write 'Stella's Birthday, 1720'?

6. Which poet wrote the poem 'The Village'?

7. In which poem does the following appear: 'Could poets or could painters fix / How angels look at thirty-six'?

8. In which century was the poem/prayer 'St Patrick's Breastplate' written?

9. In which language was 'St Patrick's Breastplate' written?

10. When was Seamus Heaney born?

11. By what other name is 'St Patrick's Breastplate' known?

12. What is Seamus Heaney's full name?

13. Who wrote the poem 'Ulster 1912'?

14. Who wrote the epic satirical poem 'The Midnight Court'?

15. Which Irish writer penned a poem entitled 'Universal Beauty'?

16. In which poem does WB Yeats write 'my countrymen Kiltartan's poor'?

17. Who wrote 'The Fiddler of Dooney'?

18. Of what materials was Yeats' 'small cabin' constructed?

19. Which Yeats poem provided the lyrics for a popular song?

20. Who wrote 'Romantic Ireland's dead and gone'?

Answers to Quiz 19

1. Oliver Goldsmith
2. 'Poem'
3. Louis MacNeice
4. 'The Village'
5. English
6. Oliver Goldsmith
7. 'Stella's Birthday, 1720'
8. 8th century
9. Irish
10. 13th April 1939
11. 'The Deer's Cry'
12. Seamus Justin Heaney
13. Rudyard Kipling
14. Brian Merriman
15. Henry Brooke
16. 'An Irish Airman Foresees His Death'
17. WB Yeats
18. 'clay and wattles'
19. 'Down By The Salley Gardens'
20. WB Yeats, in 'September 1913'

1. Who faced the death penalty or enslavement in the West Indies if found east of the river Shannon after 1st May 1654?

2. What happened to the land 'freed' by the drastic declaration of May 1654?

3. Why is *phytophthora infestans* feared in Ireland?

4. When was Ireland's second university formed?

5. Which Queen's colleges made up Ireland's second university?

6. What was the title of Ireland's second university?

7. What is Rockabill?

8. Shackleton was famously ice-bound in which aptly-named ship?

9. What is unusual about the 'Electric Brae' in Co. Down?

10. Which garment would a banshee be seen washing at a stream?

11. What was the usual, cruel form of punishment for an Irish chief who had been defeated in battle?

12. Buried in Killimer, Co. Clare, how did the 'Colleen Bawn' die?

13. What gave Bloody Foreland in Donegal its name?

14. What are the Knockmealdowns?

15. What separates the the two 'gaelic' languages?

16. Which goddess was claimed by the Tuatha de Danaan?

17. Who is Ireland's 'King Arthur'?

18. What was hunted on St Stephen's Day?

19. What were 'Cornys'?

20. In the 1840s and '50s, who or what were termed 'the Pope's Brass Band'?

1. Irish landowners

2. It was settled by Cromwell's forces

3. It is the Latin term for 'potato blight'

4. 1850

5. Queen's Colleges of Galway, Cork and Belfast

6. The Queen's University

7. A double-peaked islet with a lighthouse along Ireland's south coast

8. *Endurance*

9. An optical illusion makes it appear that objects run uphill, contrary to gravity

10. A shroud or winding-sheet

11. Blinding by needle

12. She was strangled (or drowned in the Shannon) at her husband John Scanlan's orders, in 1819

13. Its ruddy (red-tinged) sunsets

14. Mountains in Co. Waterford

15. The Irish Sea – Scots 'gallic' and Irish 'gaelic'

16. Danu

17. Arthur Guinness

18. Wrens

19. Certificates of pardon for surrendering United Irishmen, signed by Lord Cornwallis

20. Irish MPs in the British House of Commons

1. Who won the 1886 Senior Hurling Championship?

2. When was the first RDS Horse Show?

3. Who was known as the Prince of Hurling?

4. Which two Irish soccer players with the same surname ended their international careers against the same side, seven years apart?

5. For which English football team did Liam Brady most famously play?

6. Which sport first held Compromise Rules Series' with Gaelic football?

7. Which sport was demonstrated by Ireland and Germany in 1908 Olympics?

8. Where is the Hogan Stand?

9. By what margin did Munster defeat the All Blacks on 31st October 1978?

10. Of which sport was Rinty Monaghan a famous practitioner?

11. Which organisation owns Lansdowne Road stadium in Dublin?

12. Who was the first Irishman to win the Wimbledon tennis championship?

13. When did international showjumping begin at RDS (Ballsbridge)?

14. For which English football teams did David O'Leary play?

15. In which Olympics was John McNally a winner?

16. In which Olympics did Ireland first gain a bantamweight Bronze medal?

17. In which year did Frederick Gilroy win Olympic Bronze?

18. At which weights did Frederick Gilroy and Anthony Byrne win Bronze medals in the Olympics?

19. Frederick Tiedt won which Olympic boxing Silver medal?

20. Which Olympic events did John Boland win in 1896?

1. It was unfinished, due to USA invasion by GAA athletes

2. 1864

3. Lory Meagher

4. Liam and Ronnie Whelan, 1957 and 1964 against England

5. Arsenal

6. Australian Rules Football

7. Bicycle Polo

8. Croke Park

9. 12-0

10. Boxing

11. Irish Rugby Football Union

12. Joshua Pim, 1893

13. 1926

14. Arsenal, Leeds

15. 1952, Silver medal

16. 1956

17. 1956

18. Bantamweight and Lightweight

19. Welterweight

20. Tennis singles, and doubles with a German competitor

1. Who was Ireland's second President?

2. For which international organisation of states does Ireland provide armed forces?

3. How long is an Irish Presidential term?

4. Who stood for election in 1828 as 'Man of the People'?

5. Which Prime Minister of New Zealand, born in Co. Derry 1856, almost shared his name with a tractor?

6. Where did Dáil Éireann first assemble?

7. When did Dáil Éireann first assemble?

8. Which post did James Chichester-Clarke hold in 1969?

9. Who wrote "to my beloved son, John Redmond"?

10. Which political party did William Joyce co-found in England?

11. Edward Carson was first elected to Parliament for which constituency?

12. Who founded the Fenian Brotherhood secret society?

13. Who founded the Progressive Democrats?

14. To which movement was the Ulster Solemn League and Covenant in 1912 in opposition?

15. What was the duration of the first Northern Ireland Assembly?

16. Which political party did de Valera form in 1926?

17. What does 'Fianna Fail' mean in English?

18. Who introduced the first Irish Home Rule Bill?

19. Which Irish President was elected by the largest margin?

20. Who founded the Fenian Brotherhood in US?

1. Sean T O'Kelly

2. United Nations

3. Seven years

4. Daniel O'Connell

5. William Ferguson Massey – Massey Ferguson is a tractor manufacturer

6. Round room of Dublin's Mansion House

7. 21st January 1919

8. Prime Minister of Northern Ireland

9. Pope Pius X, 27th April 1905

10. National Socialist League

11. Dublin University

12. John O'Mahony

13. Mary Harney and Des O'Malley

14. Home Rule for Ireland

15. Seventy-two days

16. Fianna Fail

17. 'Soldiers of Destiny'

18. William Gladstone

19. Mary McAleese

20. Colonel John O'Mahony (1815-77)

1. On which island in Lough Derg is St Patrick's Purgatory?

2. What is the county town of Leitrim?

3. Where is Port Erin?

4. What were transmitted and received from 16th October 1907, at Clifden in Co. Galway?

5. Dun Laoghaire was once known by which less Gaelic name?

6. Where was Charles Stewart Parnell born?

7. Where was St Brendan born?

8. In which county is Lough Kee?

9. The Ardigeen River flows through which county?

10. Where did Robert the Bruce take refuge after his defeat, and learn to 'try and try again' from the spider in his cave?

11. What is the closest country to the Republic of Ireland, politically?

12. How many Provinces were there in medieval times?

13. What was the capital of the ancient Province of North Leinster?

14. Where is Slemish mountain?

15. Where was the Fenian Brotherhood founded?

16. Name the first three Glens of Antrim (in alphabetical order).

17. Which Tipperary hills once contained coal deposits?

18. What was the former name of Randalstown, Co. Antrim?

19. What is the origin of the name Tara, Co. Meath?

20. Where was Catherine, second wife of 12th Earl of Desmond born?

1. Station Island

2. Carrick-on-Shannon

3. Isle of Man, in the Irish Sea

4. Transatlantic wireless telegrams

5. Kingstown

6. Avondale, Co. Wicklow

7. Fenit, near Tralee, in 483AD

8. Roscommon

9. Cork

10. Rathlin Island

11. Northern Ireland

12. Five

13. Temuir, better known as Tara

14. In the north of Co. Antrim

15. New York

16. Glenaan, Glenariff, Glenarm

17. Slieveardagh Hills

18. Mainwater

19. Royal acropolis

20. Villierstown, Co. Waterford

1. How many Apprentice Boys shut Derry's gates?

2. When was the Siege of Derry lifted?

3. How did Patrick Sarsfield, created Earl of Lucan in 1691, die?

4. What were the '£10' castles?

5. How far behind was DMT (Dublin Mean Time) from GMT (Greenwich Mean Time)?

6. What were the dimensions of the £10 castles?

7. How long did the 'Siege of Derry' last?

8. Which navies fought a battle off Castletownshend, Cork in 1602?

9. Who became Earl of Ulster in 1205?

10. Name the first turbine-engined vessel to cross the Atlantic.

11. Who landed 1000 men at Killala, Co. Mayo in 1798?

12. Which organisations fought the 'Battle of the Diamond'?

13. What is the origin of Swords, Co. Dublin?

14. In which year did St Patrick's Day become a Bank Holiday?

15. What name was Patrick Sarsfield given on being knighted?

16. In 1446, what marked 'an Irish enemy'?

17. Which unwelcome visitor arrived in Ireland in 1348?

18. How did Strongbow die, according to the Four Masters?

19. At the time of Queen Elizabeth I, where was 'the most perilous place in all the isle'?

20. What did French General Humbert establish in Ireland in 1798?

1. Thirteen

2. 28th July 1689

3. While fighting for France against William of Orange at the battle of Landen, Flanders

4. Castles built from 1429 in the Pale area of Ireland, with £10 grant from government

5. 25 minutes behind Greenwich

6. 20 feet in length 16 feet in width and 40 feet in height or more

7. 105 days

8. English and Spanish navies

9. Hugh de Lacy

10. *Victorian*

11. General Humbert, of France

12. Protestant 'Peep O'Day Boys', and Catholic 'Defenders'

13. St Columbkille's Well (sórd means 'well')

14. 1902

15. Earl of Lucan

16. Any man with an unshaven upper lip

17. The Black Death

18. 'of an ulcer, which had broken out on his foot'

19. The province of Ulster

20. A Provisional Government

1. Which rugby personality's biography was self-described as "20 per cent… about rugby… 80 per cent is pornography"?

2. Who was the first archbishop of Dublin in 1162?

3. What was the nickname of snooker champion Alex Higgins?

4. Wolfe Tone is a famous 18th-century figure. What was his first name?

5. Who was the Red Earl of Ulster?

6. Which religious Order was founded by Edmund Burke's mother?

7. A Gore-Booth motto runs 'quod ero spero'. What does this Latin phrase mean?

8. In 1861, what percentage of the population of Western Australia was Irish?

9. When did the novelist Lady Morgan die?

10. Who said "We are fighting for bread and butter"?

11. Who said that sex "never came to Ireland until Teilifís Éireann went on the air"?

12. Who addressed members of the Dáil in 1963: "…if your own President had never left Brooklyn, he might be standing up here instead of me"?

13. Which Taoiseach's daughter became a famous novelist and TV producer?

14. What was Grace O'Malley's feared title?

15. Who was the architect of Dublin's General Post Office?

16. Who began the successful east-west flight across the Atlantic from Ireland in 1928?

17. Bernardo O'Higgins is known as?

18. Which Irishman won the Nobel Peace Prize in 1974?

19. What was the calling of Donagh, son of Thomas McDonagh?

20. What was Hugh O'Neill also known as?

1. Mick Doyle

2. St Laurence O'Toole

3. Hurricane

4. Theobald

5. Richard de Burgo, a Norman

6. Presentation Order

7. 'I hope what I shall be'

8. 21.30%

9. 1859

10. James Larkin

11. Oliver J Flanagan, Fine Gael TD, March 1966

12. American President, John Fitzgerald Kennedy

13. Cecilia Ahern, daughter of Bertie Ahern

14. Pirate Queen

15. Francis Johnston

16. Baron von Hunefeld, Captain Koehl, Colonel Fitzmaurice

17. The 'Liberator of Chile'

18. Sean MacBride

19. He was a poet

20. The Sugane Earl

1. How is Lennox Robinson best remembered?

2. What is The Lios?

3. Which organisation did Richard Martin help found?

4. The 'discoverer' of the potato, Sir Walter Raleigh, introduced which other famous plant to Europe?

5. In which year was 'Bloomsday' first marked with a week of celebration?

6. Why is 'Bloomsday' so-called?

7. After whom were the 4th-century Irish Fenian warriors named?

8. What are 'Mass Rocks'?

9. What is another name for the Great Skellig?

10. What does the acronym GUBU stand for?

11. Where would you find 'Seven Heads'?

12. Which Kilkenny great house, burned down in 1922, shares its name with the greatest American festival of the 1960s?

13. Why was part of Carlow Castle demolished in the 1880s?

14. Prior to the introduction of the Euro, what was the unit of currency in Ireland?

15. Who or what was 'Roaring Meg'?

16. What is Ireland's Eye?

17. What is Dundrod, Co. Antrim, famous for?

18. According to the song, to what should you 'treat your Mary-Anne'?

19. Where might you find 'Finn MacCool's Fingers'?

20. What, after potatoes, is the main ingredient of champ?

1. Dramatist
2. An ancient stone circle
3. Royal Society for the Prevention of Cruelty to Animals
4. Tobacco
5. 1962
6. The main character in Joyce's *Ulysses*, Leopold Bloom, begins his odyssey through Dublin on this date
7. Finn MacCool
8. Catholic religious services were curtailed, so Mass was said in out-of-the-way fields, using rocks as altars
9. Skellig Michael
10. 'grotesque, unprecedented, bizarre and unique'
11. West of Clonakilty Bay, Cork
12. Woodstock
13. As part of an ill-advised extension programme – too much gunpowder was used
14. The punt
15. A cannon in Derry during its long siege
16. A small island north of Howth in Co. Dublin
17. Motor racing and motorcycle circuit
18. Dulse and yellowman
19. Shantemon Hill, Cavan, Co. Cavan
20. Scallions, spring onions

1. Which Formula One motor-racing team featured Eddie Irvine, on his retirement from the sport in 2002?

2. Which sport which originated in Ireland is also an offence in soccer?

3. St George McCarthy was a founder member of the GAA, and a member of which other organisation?

4. What distinction does sportsman Kevin Moran hold?

5. How many times did Kevin Moran receive his distinctive sporting honour?

6. Which rugby clubs play at Lansdowne Road?

7. Who won his first Grand National in 2000?

8. Which northern Rugby legend led the British Lions in 1974?

9. For which English football teams did Frank Stapleton play?

10. Which sport does Darren Clarke play?

11. Padraig Harrington missed out on a golf championship in 2000 for what unusual reason?

12. Where was Willie John McBride born?

13. Which Irish-trained horse did Ruby Walsh ride to Grand National victory?

14. Who trained the 153rd Grand National winner in 2000?

15. What is the connection between trainer and rider of Papillon?

16. What is the connection between the winning horses in the 1999 and 2000 Grand National races?

17. What is unusual about the winner and runner-up in the 1998 Irish Grand National?

18. Which horse won the Grand National in 1998?

19. In which sport was John J Flanagan (1873-1938) famous?

20. In which event did Ronnie Delaney win Olympic Gold?

1. Jaguar

2. Handball

3. The RIC

4. Only man ever to win both All-Ireland medal (gaelic football) and FA Cup medal (Manchester United)

5. Twice GAA (1976-77) FA (1983, 85)

6. Wanderers and Lansdowne

7. Ruby Walsh

8. Willie John McBride

9. Arsenal, Derby County, Blackburn Rovers, Huddersfield Town, Bradford City

10. Golf

11. He forgot to sign his tournament score card, invalidating his play

12. Moneyglass, near Toomebridge, Co. Antrim

13. Papillon

14. Ted Walsh

15. Father and son

16. They were both trained and ridden by father-son teams

17. Winner won Grand National in 1999, runner-up won Grand National in 2000

18. Bobbyjo

19. Hammer-throw

20. 1500 metres

1. Which two constituencies were held by Eoin MacNeill in the first Dáil?

2. What is the English translation of Fine Gael?

3. Who was the first leader of the SDLP?

4. Who formed Fianna Fail?

5. What was Taoiseach Jack Lynch's less well-known second name?

6. Which Irishman became President of Israel?

7. When was the Progressive Democrat party formed in Ireland?

8. Where was Douglas Hyde, future Irish President, born?

9. What was notable about the Ulster Solemn League and Covenant in 1912?

10. Which Irish President could be described as Hispano-Celtic?

11. What is the minimum age of an Irish president?

12. How many times was Charles Haughey Irish Prime Minister?

13. Who did Mary McAleese 'defeat' in the Presidential election?

14. What is the English translation of Fianna Fail?

15. What was "the best machine...for governing a country against its will"?

16. Who said this "...whatever happens, my own countrymen won't kill me"?

17. When did Michael Collins die?

18. Who described de Valera as a "Spanish onion"?

19. Which party did David Trimble lead for 10 years until 2005?

20. When did Charles Haughey become Taoiseach for a third term?

1. Derry City and the National University of Ireland

2. 'Tribe of the Gaels'

3. Gerry Fitt, later Lord Fitt

4. Éamon de Valera

5. Mary

6. Chaim Herzog

7. 2nd January 1986

8. Frenchpark, Co. Roscommon

9. Many people signed in their own blood

10. Éamon de Valera: Irish mother, Spanish father

11. Thirty-five years of age

12. Three

13. Mary Banotti

14. 'Warriors of Destiny'

15. Dublin Castle

16. Michael Collins, 18th August 1922

17. 22nd August 1922, in an ambush by his 'own countrymen'

18. JH Thomas, Dominions Secretary, 1931

19. UUP

20. 10th March 1987

1. Where was the first 'Irish Republic'?

2. Who was the President of Humbert's 'Republic'?

3. In 1798, who was the Knight of Kerry?

4. When and where was 'Lord Haw-Haw' executed?

5. Which Irish writer wrote scripts for Lord Haw-Haw?

6. How did Wolfe Tone die?

7. What is unusual about Ireland's Nobel Peace prize winners?

8. Two men of which name suffered opposite fates 'for Ireland'?

9. Which medal was awarded to the RUC in April 2000?

10. What was the name of the first US-commissioned warship, which John Barry captained?

11. Who landed in Dingle Bay in 1579, leading a Munster rebellion?

12. Which international figure financed many of the soldiers taking part in the 1579 Munster expedition?

13. What date was the Easter Rising?

14. Who stole the Crown Jewels from the Tower of London in May 1671?

15. Who, after his death, was described as "the destroyer of Ireland in general"?

16. The 5th Earl of Donegall owned land around which area in late 1760s?

17. When was the RIC disbanded?

18. When was Ireland's first department store opened?

19. When was the first electric tramway in the British Isles opened?

20. Who is the famous partner of William Hare?

1. The area around Killala, Connaught in 1798

2. John Moore

3. Maurice Fitzgerald

4. 3rd January 1946 in London

5. Francis Stuart

6. He slit his own throat in prison

7. The award has always been shared (1974, 1977, 1998)

8. Erskine Childers

9. The George Cross, for valour

10. United States

11. Sir James Fitzmaurice

12. Pope Gregory XIII

13. Monday 24th April 1916

14. Colonel Thomas Blood, 1618-80

15. Edward Bruce

16. Belfast

17. 12th August 1922

18. 9th August 1922

19. 1883, between Portrush and Bushmills, Co. Antrim

20. William Burke, Cork (Burke and Hare)

1. What does 'ban' mean in Irish?

2. What was Bord Fáilte?

3. What was an 'aenach'?

4. What does 'saoirse' mean?

5. What was 'caid'?

6. What is 'Domnach'?

7. What does 'Aibréan' mean?

8. What does 'Mean Fómhair' mean?

9. What is 'Mí na Nollaig'?

10. What is 'hurling' in Irish?

11. What is a 'camán'?

12. What is 'Seanad Éireann'?

13. What does 'gorm' mean in Irish?

14. What were the 'sidhe'?

15. Who or what is De Danaan?

16. What was Teampall Mór?

17. What does the slogan 'Erin Go Bragh' mean?

18. What is Irish for 'deer'?

19. What is the 'shanvanvocht'?

20. What is 'horse' in Irish?

Answers to Quiz 30

1. White
2. The Irish Tourist Board (now Fáilte Ireland)
3. An expanse of grass on which fairs and gatherings took place
4. Freedom
5. An early Irish team ball-game
6. Sunday
7. April
8. September
9. December
10. Iománaíocht
11. A hurley stick
12. Irish Senate
13. Blue
14. Fairy folk (pronounced 'shee')
15. An Irish folk group
16. The Cathedral of Derry
17. 'Ireland for ever'
18. Fia
19. 'Sean Bhean Vocht' or 'poor old woman' – Ireland in the 19th century
20. Capall

1. Percy French wrote about which Eastern figure?

2. Who wrote the opera *Duenna*?

3. What is the real name of U2's 'Bono'?

4. What band of a similar name did Shane MacGowan (ex-Pogues) form?

5. What is Chris de Burgh's real name?

6. Neil Hannon, of the 'Divine Comedy', takes his name from which Italian poet's work?

7. 'The Ballad of Owen Roe' concerns which Irish noble?

8. Which poet wrote the unofficial Irish anthem 'A Nation Once Again'?

9. When did The Rolling Stones first play in Ireland?

10. What action do the Mourne Mountains accomplish, according to the famous song by Percy French?

11. Name the members of U2.

12. Which members of U2 are not Irish-born?

13. Which Irish groups featured members of the Lynch family?

14. Which boy band achieved a record seven No.1s with their first seven singles?

15. Sinead O'Connor was once known by which other, 'religious' name?

16. Who is the singer-songwriter brother of Irish singer-songwriter Luka Bloom?

17. Which ballad contains the line "For the sake of my religion I was forced to leave my native home"?

18. Which song of *Father Ted*'s Dougal was written by Neil 'Divine Comedy' Hannon?

19. Which Irish singer-songwriter is most famous for 'Lady in Red'?

20. Where was flautist James Galway born?

1. 'Abdul Abulbul Ameer'

2. Richard Brinsley Sheridan

3. Paul Hewson

4. The Popes

5. Christopher Davidson

6. Dante Alighieri

7. Owen Roe O'Neill (1590-1649)

8. Thomas Osborne Davis (1814-45)

9. 7th January 1965

10. "sweep down to the sea"

11. Bono, The Edge, Adam Clayton, Larry Mullen

12. Adam Clayton and The Edge

13. Boyzone, B*witched, Buffalo G

14. Westlife

15. Mother Bernadette Mary

16. Christy Moore

17. 'The Banished Defender'

18. 'My Lovely Horse'

19. Chris de Burgh

20. Belfast

1. Who wrote *A Modest Proposal*?

2. Which satirical novel sounds like a wildlife documentary?

3. Who was the first Irish winner of the Booker Prize?

4. Who wrote an *Argument against abolishing Christianity*?

5. To which 'Hidden Ireland' did Daniel Corkery refer?

6. What is the name of the estate in Colleen McCullough's *Thorn Birds*?

7. Which Co. Dublin town is the setting for Sheridan le Fanu's
   The House By The Churchyard?

8. Which American writer of the *Pern* novels became an Irish citizen?

9. Flann O'Brien is the novel-writing pseudonym of which Irish author?

10. What was author Martin Ross' real name?

11. Which novelist wrote the book on which the film *The Snapper* is based?

12. Who wrote *Leaves from a Prison Diary*?

13. Which Irish writer was grant funded by Royal Literary Fund in 1915?

14. Who wrote *Soggarth Aroon* in 1831?

15. What was the subject of *Soggarth Aroon*?

16. Where was author William Trevor Cox born?

17. Whose autobiography was entitled *An Only Child*?

18. What was Irish novelist Somerville's first name?

19. When was *Dublin University Magazine* first published?

20. To which city according to one author does the description 'strumpet' apply?

1. Jonathan Swift

2. *At Swim-Two-Birds*

3. Iris Murdoch

4. Jonathan Swift

5. Munster, in the 18th century

6. Drogheda

7. Chapelizod

8. Anne McCaffrey

9. Brian O'Nolan

10. Violet Martin (Ross from her home, Ross House)

11. Roddy Doyle

12. Michael Davitt

13. James Joyce

14. Novelist John Banim

15. Irish priests

16. Mitchelstown, Co. Cork

17. Short-story writer Frank O'Connor

18. Edith

19. 1833

20. Dublin

1. Which Irish scientist could be credited with discovering 'blue-sky thinking'?

2. What entertainment did James Joyce and partners provide from December 20th 1909?

3. How long was the first steam ship voyage across the Atlantic?

4. Which shorthand inventor was born in Rockcorry, Co. Monaghan?

5. What was the principal industry of Sion Mills in Tyrone until the 21st century?

6. What product is produced by a company headquartered at Tandragee Castle?

7. Who was reputed to be the owner of Ireland's first petrol-driven motor car?

8. What was the Nobel 2000?

9. What was JB Dunlop's occupation?

10. Which sister ship of *Titanic* had an equally 'striking' history?

11. What did Belfast's Hickson's shipyard become in 1861?

12. In 1911, what were the three largest ships in the world?

13. What tonnage was each of 1911's largest ocean-going vessels?

14. Early in 2000, Ireland was named the world's largest exporter of which commodity?

15. What did John DeLorean set up in Co. Antrim during the 1980s?

16. Which type of pottery is produced in Belleek?

17. Which company popularised Ferguson's tractor?

18. Which crop does Bessy Bell harvest year-round?

19. What was unusual about the bodywork of a classic DeLorean car?

20. What make of car did Dr Colohan own in the 19th century?

1. John Tyndall. Born in Leighlinbridge, Co. Carlow in 1820, his theories on light diffraction by dust and large molecules offered an explanation of the sky's 'blue' appearance.

2. They opened the first cinema in Dublin, the Volta

3. Nineteen days

4. John R Gregg

5. Linen

6. Potato crisps

7. Dr John Colohan, of Blackrock, Co. Dublin

8. A bubble car produced under license in Co. Down

9. Veterinary Surgeon

10. Olympic

11. Harland & Wolff

12. *Britannic, Olympic, Titanic*

13. 46,000 tons

14. Computer software

15. The DeLorean Motor Company

16. Parian china

17. Massey-Ferguson

18. Electricity from wind energy. There is a wind farm situated on Bessy Bell mountain in Co. Tyrone.

19. The metal bodywork was not painted

20. Benz Velo, bought in 1896

1. Which Alan Parker film featured a group of Dublin teenagers forming a band?

2. Which film featured Bronagh Gallagher alongside Eric Stoltz and John Travolta?

3. Bronagh Gallagher featured in which film where she carried Liam Neeson?

4. Which film featured Liam Neeson as a character with a 'dark' side?

5. Which film featured the lead singer of Irish band The Corrs, and Madonna?

6. Which film features Ewan McGregor as an iconic Irish novelist?

7. Liam Neeson spars with Christian Bale in which film by Christoper Nolan?

8. Which American film famously features Van Morrison's song 'Moondance'?

9. Where was the film *Excalibur* principally filmed?

10. Brendan Gleeson appeared in which film as a police inspector on the trail of two Dublin runaways?

11. Gabriel Byrne appears as a master criminal in which film?

12. Which two films of 1999 starred Gabriel Byrne on either side of good and evil?

13. In which film did Brendan Gleeson appear alongside Mel Gibson, not as an Irishman, but a Scot?

14. Cyril Cusack starred in Francois Truffaut's film of which Ray Bradbury story?

15. Which Irish actress was 'Jane' to Johnny Weissmuller's *Tarzan* from the 1930s?

16. John Boorman directed Brendan Gleeson in which film based on the life of a 'colourful' Dublin criminal?

17. What was unusual about John Boorman's 1998 Irish 'gangster' film?

18. Which Irish band of the 1960s takes its name from a 1950s American science fiction film about giant ants?

19. James Mason, as a weary member of 'the Organisation', is wounded in a botched robbery in which Carol Reed film?

20. Victor McLaglen appeared in a 1935 film by John Ford, from a novel involving 'the Organisation'. What was its title?

Answers to Quiz 34

1. *The Commitments*

2. *Pulp Fiction*

3. *Star Wars: Episode One*

4. *Darkman*

5. *Evita*, directed by Alan Parker

6. *Nora*

7. *Batman Begins*

8. *An American Werewolf in London*

9. Ardmore Studios

10. *Into The West*

11. *The Usual Suspects*

12. *Stigmata* and *End of Days* as, respectively a priest and the Devil

13. *Braveheart*

14. *Fahrenheit 451*

15. Maureen O'Sullivan

16. *The General*

17. It was shot in black and white

18. Them

19. *Odd Man Out*

20. *The Informer*

1. On which infamous murder did Gerald Griffin base *The Collegians*?

2. The motorcycling Dunlop brothers shared which distinction with a famous Belfast vet?

3. What is the significance of Harriet Shaw Weaver to Irish literature?

4. In 1847 who was described as 'a feeble old man muttering from a table'?

5. Who was awarded the Nobel Prize for Physics along with Irish physicist Ernest Walton in 1951?

6. Who was Michael Collins' fiancée?

7. Where was Harry Ferguson born?

8. Who formed the Brothers of the Christian Schools (Christian Brothers)?

9. For which church was Richard Whately Archbishop of Dublin?

10. Which business was the Countess of Desart responsible for?

11. What was the name of the computer software company founded by Dave Perry?

12. To whom does the film title *Nora* refer?

13. Sean MacBride, joint winner of the 1974 Nobel Peace Prize, was son to which famous Irish nationalist and literary inspiration?

14. Who was Sweeney Menn?

15. Which Irishman and Canadian Minister for Agriculture was assassinated?

16. What is John Philip Holland credited with?

17. Who was 'Sir' Dan Donnelly?

18. Who was 'Devil Dill'?

19. What nationality was Robert Flaherty, documentary film-maker?

20. Who termed the Aran Islands "Three stepping stones out of Europe"?

1. John Scanlan's murder of his wife, 'The Colleen Bawn'

2. They were all three famous for their work on pneumatic tyres: JB Dunlop patented them; Robert and Joey Dunlop raced on them

3. She was James Joyce's benefactor, supporting his writing with funds

4. Daniel O'Connell

5. Sir John D Cockcroft

6. Kitty Kiernan

7. Gromwell, Hillsborough, Co. Down

8. Edmund Ignatius Rice

9. Church of Ireland

10. Kilkenny Woollen Mills

11. Shiny Entertainment

12. Nora Barnacle, James Joyce's wife

13. Maud Gonne (MacBride)

14. Monarch of Ireland, 616-628AD

15. Thomas D'Arcy McGee, 1825-68

16. Inventing a workable submarine

17. A boxer, born 1788

18. John Greer Dill, World War II Field Marshal

19. American

20. Seamus Heaney

1. Lough Derg is a pilgrimage site for which Saint?

2. Who was once known as the 'first Patrick'?

3. St Brendan most commonly referred to as?

4. The Cross of Cong, fashioned *c.* 1125 in Roscommon, was made to house which relic?

5. Which Co. Cavan bishop first translated the Bible into Irish?

6. Which medieval Order once maintained a base in Ross Carbery, Co. Cork?

7. Which Pope first forbade the pilgrimages to St Patrick's Purgatory?

8. Which saint was said to have cursed Tara?

9. Tara was damaged in the 19th century in a fruitless search for which religious artefact?

10. When is the feast day of St Brendan?

11. Complete the 17th-century phrase: 'If there were no priests, there would be no…'?

12. When did St Fergal die?

13. When was Kilcooly Abbey founded?

14. When was the *Messiah* first performed?

15. Which cleric ordained singer Sinead O'Connor a priest?

16. From which precious metal was the Ardagh Chalice fashioned?

17. Which 'relic' of St Oliver Plunkett, an Irish bishop executed in England, survives?

18. Where is the most famous relic of St Oliver Plunkett to be found?

19. Who was the first papal legate to Ireland?

20. Pope Adrian VI granted Ireland to which English king in 1155?

1. Saint Patrick

2. Bishop Palladius

3. The Navigator

4. A fragment of 'the true Cross'

5. Bedell, in the 17th century

6. The Knights Templar

7. Pope Alexander VI, 1497

8. St Ruadhan of Lorrha

9. The Ark of the Covenant

10. 16th May

11. 'Wolves'. In 1650, an anti-clerical syllogism (a piece of subtle, deceptive reasoning) ran: 'priests are the cause of all Ireland's woes; wolves are a misery; therefore priests are to blame for the existence of wolves'

12. 784AD

13. 1184

14. 13th April 1742

15. Bishop Michael Cox

16. Gold

17. His head

18. In a shrine at St Peter's Church, Drogheda, Co. Louth

19. Cardinal Paparo, 1150

20. Henry II, by a proclamation 'Laudabiliter'

1. What is Irish Mist?

2. What is 'a wake'?

3. What status did UNESCO confer on the Giant's Causeway?

4. Which is the larger Neolithic monument: Newgrange or Knowth?

5. Where would you find the Bull, Heifer and Cow?

6. To which post was Mrs Mary Westby appointed in 1760?

7. What was Haulbowline?

8. What was a 'nickey'?

9. What first appeared in public on Kingstown's East Pier in 1852?

10. What is unusual about the 1920s yacht *Saoirse*?

11. Which Irish lawyer is famous for prosecuting a playwright, and defending a school boy over the alleged theft of a postal order?

12. Who said of whom, regarding a famous legal battle: "No doubt he will pursue his case with all the added bitterness of an old friend"?

13. What was created in Doohulla, Connemara in 1854?

14. What is notable about Dublin's Rotunda hospital?

15. What were 'Suffolk Fencibles' and 'Ancient Britons'?

16. What was described as 'this noble weapon glittering above us'?

17. What is *Chondrus crispus*?

18. What was the 'Leviathan of Parsonstown'?

19. What was first set on a Dublin sandbar in 1735?

20. Why is Pigeon House so-called?

1. A mixture of Irish whiskey and honey

2. A celebration of the life of the deceased

3. World Heritage Site

4. Newgrange: it is 2 metres higher and 10 metres larger in diameter

5. Off Dursey Head (they are islets)

6. Keeper of Loop Head lighthouse

7. A Cork naval base, completed in 1894

8. A Co. Down fishing vessel

9. The anemometer

10. It was the first vessel to carry the Irish tricolour around the world

11. Sir Edward Carson. He successfully prosecuted Oscar Wilde, and was defence counsel in the legal case brought to the theatre by playwright Terence Rattigan as 'The Winslow Boy'.

12. Oscar Wilde, of Edward Carson. Both men had attended Trinity College, Dublin.

13. The first artificial salmon river

14. First maternity hospital in Great Britain or Ireland, 1757

15. 18th-century English militias in Ireland

16. The Irish tricolour

17. Carrigeen moss

18. A telescope

19. A lightship, to warn of dangerous waters

20. After John Pidgeon, caretaker of works on the South Wall

1. When did Michelle Smith win her first Olympic swimming Gold?

2. Which early 20th-century Irish soccer international shares his name with an English snooker player?

3. For which English football teams did Pat Jennings play?

4. How many boxing medals did Ireland win in the 1952 Olympics?

5. Who trained and rode Bobbyjo?

6. What distinction does trainer Ted Walsh hold as a jockey?

7. Which 'Grand' horse race did Jonjo O'Neill never win, either as trainer or jockey?

8. In which sport have Neil Booth and Jeremy Henry represented Ireland?

9. Darren Clarke won World Match Play in 2000 by beating which golfer?

10. For which American soccer side did George Best play in 1976?

11. Tony McCoy set which world record in the 1997-98 season?

12. How is Irish golfer Christy O'Connor Snr related to Irish golfer Christy O'Connor Jnr?

13. Trinity College, Dublin's rugby club holds which distinction?

14. When was Trinity's rugby club officially founded?

15. In which Olympic Games did Ronnie Delaney win Olympic Gold?

16. How many Olympic medals was Michelle Smith awarded in 1996?

17. With which two teams did the 1972 All Blacks touring side draw in Ireland?

18. Which team won the 1972 Five Nations?

19. Which Irish soccer international began and ended his career against Belgium in the 1920s and 1930s?

20. Which footballer played in only one international, in the World Cup campaign of 1937?

1. 1996

2. Jimmy White, who played in 1928 for Ireland against Belgium

3. Arsenal, Tottenham Hotspur, Watford

4. One

5. Tommy and Paul Carberry

6. He was champion Irish amateur jockey 11 times

7. The Grand National

8. Bowls

9. 'Tiger' Woods

10. San Jose Earthquakes

11. He rode 253 winners in a riding season

12. Uncle and nephew

13. It is the second oldest rugby club in the world

14. 1854

15. Melbourne, Australia, 1956

16. Four (three Gold, one Bronze)

17. Munster and the Ireland side

18. No one – it was declared 'no result' due to travel complications – the Troubles

19. Joe Golding

20. Tom Arrigan

1. When was RTÉ established?

2. From which transmitter did regular TV broadcasting start in Ireland?

3. What was the first RTÉ 'soap opera'?

4. Who hosted *The Late Late Show* for the longest period?

5. Who took over from the first presenter of *The Late Late Show*?

6. Which long-running game-show did Irish comedian Roy Walker present?

7. Which actor played a villain in *Wanderly Wagon* and a wayward priest in *Father Ted*?

8. What are the two most famous aliens on Irish TV?

9. What kind of animal is Dustin?

10. Where was the series *Ballykissangel* filmed?

11. What was the name of the public house in *Ballykissangel*?

12. What was the name of the *Ballykissangel* character played by Dervla Kirwan?

13. What is Dustin's occupation?

14. Which Irish media personality has covered the Eurovision Song Contest for both RTÉ and BBC?

15. In which year did *The Late Late Show* begin?

16. Eamonn Andrews presented which television show dedicated to celebrities?

17. What is the short name of the Irish language TV station which was originally called TnaG (Teilifís na Gaeilge)?

18. On which Irish TV show did Boyzone first appear?

19. What is the name of RTÉ 'agricultural soap'?

20. When did regular TV broadcasting begin in Ireland?

1. 12th April 1960

2. Divis Mountain, Belfast

3. *Tolka Row*

4. Gay Byrne

5. Pat Kenny

6. *Catchphrase*

7. Frank Kelly

8. Zig and Zag

9. Turkey

10. Vale of Avoca, Co. Wicklow

11. Fitzgerald's

12. Assumpta Fitzgerald

13. Builder

14. Terry Wogan

15. 1962

16. *This Is Your Life*

17. TG4 (Teilifís na Gaeilge Ceathair)

18. *The Late Late Show*

19. *Glenroe*

20. 21st July 1955

1. Who introduced the word 'electron' to the English language?
2. Which theory of William Rowan Hamilton is important in quantum physics?
3. William Rowan Hamilton held which post at twenty-two years of age?
4. Which famous mathematician died in Ireland 8th December 1864, having taught at Queen's College, Cork for many years?
5. What is another name for 'dulse'?
6. Which Irish cleric is noted for his mathematical prowess?
7. Who was known as 'the father of American chemistry'?
8. What was the maximum magnification of the 'Leviathan'?
9. Which scientific post was held by 3rd Earl of Rosse from 1848-54?
10. What is the son of 3rd Earl of Rosse best remembered for?
11. Why might 1st Earl of Cork & Orrery be described as 'the grandfather of chemistry'?
12. Who was the first Astronomer Royal for Ireland?
13. Which Irish scientist mapped the earth's magnetic field?
14. When were Dublin's first zoological gardens opened?
15. Which creatures would you find at Seaforde Gardens, Portaferry?
16. What date did Archbishop Ussher ascribe to Creation?
17. Who built the 'Leviathan of Parsonstown'?
18. Which Irish scientist might have been interested in the work of Prokofiev?
19. Creevykeel in Sligo has a megalithic court cairn. What does the term 'megalithic' mean?
20. Peter Woulfe gave his name to an item of laboratory equipment. Name it.

1. George Johnstone Stoney, 1826-1911, Irish physicist

2. Theory of quaternions, 3-dimensional calculus

3. Astronomer Royal of Ireland

4. George Boole, of 'Boolean algebra' fame

5. Dillisk

6. James Ussher, Archbishop of Armagh

7. William McNeven, 1763-1841

8. 6000x

9. President of the Royal Society

10. Charles Parsons (1854-1931) invented the steam turbine

11. His seventh son, Robert Boyle, was called 'the father of chemistry'

12. John Brinkley, in 1792

13. Humphrey Lloyd, 1800-81

14. 1830

15. Butterflies from all over the world

16. 4004 BC

17. William Parsons

18. Peter Woulfe (The musical tale *Peter and the Wolf* was written by Prokofiev)

19. 'Large stone' – describing the construction of the monuments

20. The Woulfe Bottle, a two-necked glass container for safe chemical-handling

1. What did Daniel O'Connell once call Sir Robert Peel?

2. When did Bernadette Devlin make her House of Commons 'maiden speech'?

3. Which party did Garret Fitzgerald lead?

4. When did former Irish President Douglas Hyde die?

5. Which UN Commission had ex-President Mary Robinson as its head?

6. Who was Prime Minister of Northern Ireland, 1921-40?

7. Who founded Sinn Féin?

8. Who described Daniel O'Connell as 'a feeble old man'?

9. When was the first Irish Home Rule Bill introduced?

10. Who was to represent Co. Armagh in the first Dáil?

11. Where was Chaim Herzog born?

12. Which political party did John Hume lead until 2001?

13. What does UUP stand for?

14. Who founded the Home Government Association in 1870?

15. Who was the first Cork man to become Taoiseach?

16. When was the Bank of Ireland founded?

17. Who declared the following of Kinsale in 1601: 'I hold this town for Christ and the King of Spain'?

18. Who announced the American Declaration of Independence?

19. Which Irish division fought and lost 5000 men at the Battle of the Somme?

20. What became of Erskine Childers, father and son?

1. 'Orange Peel'

2. 22nd March 1969

3. Fine Gael

4. 12th July 1949

5. Human Rights

6. James Craig

7. Arthur Griffith

8. Benjamin Disraeli, British Prime Minister

9. 1886

10. Michael Collins

11. In Belfast, 1918

12. SDLP

13. Ulster Unionist Party

14. Isaac Butt

15. Jack Lynch (1917-1999)

16. 1783

17. Don Juan d'Aguila, having occupied the town

18. Charles Thomson, born in Co. Derry in 1729

19. 36th Ulster Division

20. The elder Childers was executed as a Republican in the Civil War, the younger later became President of Ireland

1. Which English magazine first serialised James Joyce's novel, *A Portrait of the Artist as a Young Man* in 1914?

2. Which songwriter and artist wrote 'The Mountains of Mourne'?

3. When was a fixed-payment system agreed for poems written by Irish bards?

4. Where was the other end of the 'wireless' telegraph from Ireland?

5. Which is Ireland's longest surviving newspaper?

6. What is Ireland's second oldest newspaper?

7. What is Ireland's third oldest newspaper?

8. Which award did actor Peter O'Toole receive from a veteran magazine in April 2000?

9. Who wrote that 'A people without a language is only half a nation'?

10. Where was the artist Francis Bacon born?

11. For which works is Francis Bacon best-remembered?

12. What is the modern name of the *West Cork Eagle and County Advertiser*?

13. What was the *West Cork Eagle*'s promotional boast?

14. Which Cork newspaper shares its name with the Antipodean counterpart of Polaris?

15. Which weekly newspaper did Thomas Osborne Davis help found?

16. Who succeeded Thomas Davis as editor of their campaigning newspaper?

17. Which poet and artist described himself as 'an Irishman of planter stock, by profession an art gallery man'?

18. Which artist was a leading producer Irish stained glass work?

19. Where did Thomas Davis write about the importance of 'National poetry'?

20. Which Irish ballet dancer founded the dance company which became the Royal Ballet?

1. *The Egoist*
2. Percy French
3. 590AD, at the Convention of All Ireland at Drumceat
4. Cape Breton, Canada
5. Belfast's *News Letter*
6. *The Derry Journal*
7. *The Impartial Reporter*
8. 'Oldie of the Year'
9. Thomas Davis
10. Dublin
11. His 'Screaming Popes', variations on a papal portrait by Velasquez
12. *Skibbereen Eagle*
13. 'The largest penny paper in the world'
14. *The Southern Star*
15. *The Nation*, in October 1842
16. John Mitchel
17. John Hewitt
18. Evie Hone
19. In *The Nation* newspaper
20. Dame Ninette De Valois

1. Which of the present-day Provinces is comprised of two of the
    ancient Provinces?

2. Domangard, 5th-century bishop and founder of Maghera, Co. Derry, gave
    his name to which mountain?

3. Name the 'middle three' Glens of Antrim (in alphabetical order).

4. The Druid's Seat and Glendruid House may be found near which area
    of Co. Dublin?

5. Off which part of the Irish coastline was the transatlantic liner *Lusitania*
    torpedoed by German submarine in 1915?

6. What is the county town of Mayo?

7. What is the county town of Longford?

8. What is the county town of Carlow?

9. What was the capital of the ancient Province of Munster?

10. Name the last three Glens of Antrim (in alphabetical order).

11. What is the county town of Waterford?

12. What is the county town of Wexford?

13. What is the county town of Cavan?

14. Through which county does the Kenmare River flow?

15. Through which city does the River Nore pass?

16. In which county is Bunratty Castle?

17. Where are the North and South Slobs?

18. Which Co. Mayo town featured in John Ford's *The Quiet Man*?

19. Of which Irish cities was President John F Kennedy given 'the Freedom' on
    his visit to Ireland in 1963?

20. Which area held "no water to drown a man, no timber to hang him and no
    soil to bury him"?

1. Leinster (from North Leinster and South Leinster)

2. Slieve Donard

3. Glenballyeamon, Glencloy, Glencorp

4. Killiney

5. Old Head of Kinsale

6. Castlebar

7. Longford

8. Carlow

9. Temuir Erann, near Ardpatrick, Limerick

10. Glendun, Glenshesk, Glentaisie

11. Waterford

12. Wexford

13. Cavan

14. Kerry

15. Kilkenny

16. Co. Clare

17. Wexford harbour

18. Cong

19. Cork, Limerick and Dublin

20. The Burren. This remark was made by one of Oliver Cromwell's officers.

1. What became of Padraig Pearse's former schoolhouse?

2. Where was the Dublin terminus of the Great Northern Railway?

3. Who was crowned King of Ireland in 1316?

4. When were the 'Peelers' formed?

5. When did Henry Grattan make his 'Declaration of Rights'?

6. Who is described in this line of verse? 'a haggard woman returned and Dublin went wild to meet her'.

7. Who said "You can't switch on peace like a light"?

8. When was the electric tramway in Co. Antrim between Portrush and Bushmills finally closed?

9. When was the University of Ulster established?

10. When was the garden at Heywood designed?

11. When did Kilkenny become a city?

12. When was a bounty of £1000 placed on the head of Hugh O'Neill?

13. According to Lord Cornwallis what was "the favourite pastime" of such militias as the 'Suffolk Fencibles' during 1798?

14. When did King James land in Ireland, prior to the Battle of the Boyne?

15. In what year was the proclamation 'The Provisional Government to the People of Ireland'?

16. Who made the proclamation of 'The Provisional Government to the People of Ireland'?

17. When did the first of Daniel O'Connell's 'monster meetings' take place at Tara?

18. When did the Irish 'tricolour' first appear?

19. Who described the Irish tricolour as a 'noble weapon'?

20. What led to Art O'Leary's death?

1. It is now a museum dedicated to Pearse

2. Amiens Street

3. Robert the Bruce, of Scotland

4. 1814, as Peace Preservation Police, fifteen years before the London force

5. Tuesday 16th April 1782

6. Constance Markiewicz

7. The Former Secretary of State for Northern Ireland, Mo Mowlam, September 1999

8. 1947

9. 1969

10. 1902

11. In 1609, with a charter from King James I

12. 1601

13. "Murder"

14. 12th March 1689, at Kinsale

15. July 1803

16. Robert Emmet

17. 15th August 1843

18. In 1848, the year of European revolution

19. John Mitchel

20. His refusal to sell his horse for £5

1. Which European city gave guitarist Gary Moore his biggest hit?

2. Where did ex-Beautiful South singer Brianna Corrigan come from?

3. Who wrote the words to the song 'My Lagan Love'?

4. According to the song, where was The Sash worn?

5. What is the real name of U2's 'The Edge'?

6. Which Prince song gave Sinead O'Connor her first world-wide hit?

7. Which Irish tenor was the subject of the film *Hear My Song*?

8. Who was the 'Wild Colonial Boy' of the song?

9. Where, according to the song, did Roddy McCorley die?

10. Chris de Burgh wrote which extra-terrestrial themed Christmas song?

11. What was the original title of the Irish 'boy-band' Westlife?

12. What was the title of Dana's entry in the Eurovision Song Contest?

13. Who wrote 'The Bells of Shandon'?

14. 'Eleven O'Clock Tick Tock' was an early single by which group?

15. Name the town which completes this song title: 'Sean South of...'?

16. Where was Irish-Australian rogue Jack Donohue born?

17. Which Irish musician was famous for her virtuosity on the harp, appearing many times on television?

18. Which group featured Paddy Moloney and Derek Bell?

19. Where did U2 first meet?

20. Of which Christian denomination did Sinead O'Connor become a priest?

1. Paris ('Parisian Walkways)'

2. Belfast, via Portstewart, Co. Derry, in the beautiful north

3. Joseph Campbell

4. Derry, Aughrim, Enniskillen and the Boyne

5. David Evans

6. 'Nothing Compares 2 U'

7. Josef Locke

8. Jack Donohue, 'Jack Duggan' in song

9. 'On the bridge of Toome', Toomebridge, Co. Antrim

10. 'A Spaceman came Travelling'

11. Westside

12. 'All Kinds of Everything'

13. 'Father Prout'

14. U2

15. Garryowen

16. Castlemaine, Kerry, 1809

17. Mary O'Hara

18. The Chieftains

19. Temple High School in Dublin

20. Latin Tridentine

1. Which Irish naval officer received the German Naval surrender at Scapa Flow in 1919?

2. For which first was James Dixon responsible in 1803?

3. Irish naval serviceman Charles David Lucas received a special medal on 26th June 1857. What was it?

4. How has the Irish forename Aoife been anglicised?

5. Who began construction of Carrickfergus castle?

6. What was boxer Dave McAuley's nickname?

7. What is the full name of WB Yeats?

8. Who wrote that 'National poetry is the very flowering of the soul'?

9. Turlough O'Carolan is more commonly known as?

10. Whose last words were "Either the wallpaper goes or I do"?

11. What was Ireland's population in 1956?

12. Which Cavan GAA star became Tánaiste in 1993?

13. Who was Jonathan Swift's literary muse, 'Vanessa'?

14. How was General 'Tim' Pile involved in World War II?

15. In which field was Jack Yeats, son of John Butler Yeats, a famous Irish figure?

16. What is the Irish motto of O'Sullivan Mór?

17. What does O'Sullivan Mór's motto mean in English?

18. What did Sub Lieutenant AWS Tisdall receive during World War One?

19. Who financed a film of JM Synge's *Riders to the Sea*?

20. What was Constance Markiewicz's maiden name?

1. Admiral of the Fleet, Earl Beatty

2. The first Mass on Australian soil. He was a Catholic priest.

3. The first ever Victoria Cross

4. Eva

5. John de Courcy

6. 'Boy'

7. William Butler Yeats

8. Thomas Davis

9. Carolan, the blind harper

10. Oscar Wilde

11. 2.9 million according to census on 1st June 1956

12. John Wilson

13. Esther Vanhomrigh, of Celbridge, Kildare

14. He commanded England's anti-aircraft defences

15. He was a greatly admired Irish artist

16. 'Lamh foistenach abu'

17. 'The gentle hand to victory'

18. The first Victoria Cross of the war awarded to an Irish navy man

19. Gracie Fields, famous English actress and singer

20. Gore-Booth

1. What was a 'Galway hooker'?

2. Who was 'A Silent Politician'?

3. According to Royal Navy Admiral Domville, who was 'a quiet little man with the courage of a lion'?

4. Why did Admiral Domville describe the "quiet little man" as lion-hearted?

5. What may be found between Twelve Pins and Ballyconneely Bay?

6. What are Barrcostello, Emlaghmore and Barrowen?

7. What, originally, was 'kelp'?

8. What icon did Cedric Gibbons design?

9. What is 'fives'?

10. In what month is the Auld Lammas Fair held in Ballycastle, Co. Antrim?

11. Which treasured article depicts 'two hands clasping a crowned heart'?

12. Which readily available type of 'food' was promoted in the satirical pamphlet of 1729 entitled *A Modest Proposal*?

13. How is Unshin better known?

14. What was Clann na Talmhan?

15. What were the 'Lays of the Western Gael'?

16. Who or what was Jammie Clinch?

17. What is the main concern of the Speleological Union of Ireland?

18. Who wrote of 'the dreary steeples of Fermanagh and Tyrone, emerging again'?

19. What is Talbot's Inch?

20. What is 'fionnadh bó'?

1. A fishing boat
2. James Stephens, Fenian leader, writing in 1862
3. Erskine Childers snr.
4. Childers made daring seaplane raids against German forces in 1914-16
5. Doohulla or Emlaghmore fishery
6. Galway loughs
7. The by-product of burning seaweed
8. The Academy Award
9. A variation on the sport of handball
10. August
11. The Claddagh Ring
12. The sale of the children of the poor as meat
13. River Arrow
14. The Farmers' Party, which ceased in 1960s
15. A collection of poems ('lays') by Sir William Ferguson
16. A 1920s rugby player
17. Ireland's caves and underground caverns
18. Winston Churchill
19. A village in Kilkenny
20. Cowhide, leather

1. Who was termed the "'Babe Ruth' of Gaelic football" in 1947?

2. How many boxing medals did Ireland win in the 1932 Olympics?

3. How many official horse racecourses are there in Ireland?

4. Which rugby club rather aptly won the first three years of the Senior Cup?

5. What is noteworthy about the 1922 Ulster Grand Prix?

6. Who won the first Ulster Grand Prix?

7. Which vehicle competed in the Ulster Grand Prix?

8. How many Olympic Gold medals did John J Flanagan win during his career?

9. How many times in the 1970s did Ireland win rugby's Five Nations Championship?

10. Of which International Rugby Board award was Keith Wood the first recipient?

11. What was Irish rugby player Ian McLauchlan's nickname?

12. In which Olympics did Hugh Russell win a boxing Bronze medal for Ireland?

13. At which weight did Hugh Russell fight in the 1980 Olympics?

14. At which weight did Dave McAuley win Silver for Ireland?

15. In which Olympics did Dave McAuley did win a Silver medal?

16. In which boxing division did Michael Carruth win Olympic Gold?

17. In which Olympics did Michael Carruth win a Gold medal?

18. In which Olympic event did Patrick O'Callaghan compete?

19. Which Newry man scored Aston Villa's winning goal in 1957's FA Cup final?

20. In which sport is the McCarthy Cup contested?

1. Peter O'Donohoe of Cavan

2. Two Gold

3. One, Silver

4. Trinity

5. The first road race to be won at over 60 mph

6. Hubert Hassall

7. Motorcycles

8. Three

9. Once

10. World Player of the Year, 2001

11. 'Mighty Mouse'

12. 1980

13. Flyweight

14. Bantamweight

15. 1992

16. Welterweight

17. 1992

18. Hammer throw, winning Olympic Gold in 1928 and 1932

19. Peter McParland

20. Hurling

1. Which title did Sir James Craig take on being elevated to the peerage?

2. Who was the first President of the Irish Free State?

3. Monica McWilliams was co-founder of which political party?

4. Which American office did Thomas Emmet, United Irishman, hold?

5. When was the SDLP formed?

6. Whose election address was given as '143 Leinster Road, Rathmines, Co. Dublin'?

7. Which Count was a Noble even before his elevation by the Pope in 1877?

8. Which politicians jointly won the Nobel Peace Prize in 1999?

9. What does SDLP stand for?

10. Which political party was led by Rev. Ian Paisley until he stood down from the leadership in 2008?

11. Which election saw the first Fianna Fail election contest?

12. On putting his name to the Anglo-Irish Treaty of 1921, who said "I have signed my own death warrant"?

13. Which northern constituency was represented for many years by Rev. Ian Paisley?

14. Which Roscommon priest was once vice-chairman of Sinn Féin?

15. When did Garret Fitzgerald first become Taoiseach?

16. How many consecutive terms may an Irish president serve?

17. Which Sinn Féin member was minister for Education in the Northern Ireland Assembly until 2002?

18. How many Westminster MPs are elected from Northern Ireland?

19. When was the IRA declared illegal in Ireland?

20. Who was to represent Co. Down in the first Dáil?

1. Lord Craigavon

2. WT Cosgrave

3. Northern Ireland Women's Coalition

4. State Attorney for New York

5. August 1970

6. Constance Markiewicz

7. George Noble Plunkett, made a Papal Count in 1877

8. John Hume and David Trimble

9. Social Democratic and Labour Party

10. DUP

11. 1927

12. Michael Collins

13. North Antrim

14. Father Michael O'Flanagan (1876-1942)

15. 30th June 1981

16. Two

17. Martin McGuinness

18. Seventeen

19. 1931

20. Éamon de Valera

1. Who wrote the book *Cal*?

2. Where was Lawrence Sterne born?

3. Which Irish author won the Whitbread Prize in 1988?

4. Brian O'Nolan is the real name of which Irish journalist / humourist?

5. What subjects do the *Book of Leinster* and the *Book of Armagh* have in common?

6. Where was Frank McCourt born?

7. Which Irish writer is best known as a Canadian citizen?

8. Which honour was author William Trevor awarded in 1977?

9. With what was Thomas Prior's 'List of the Absentees of Ireland' concerned?

10. Which James Joyce novel follows the life of Stephen Dedalus?

11. Who wrote the novel *The Collegians*?

12. Who wrote the novel *Strumpet City*?

13. According to Brendan Behan, what is "an author's first duty"?

14. Which footballer's autobiography was entitled *Attack*?

15. What, according to the title of his book, did Chevalier Jacques De Latocnaye undertake in 1796-97?

16. What has been modified in James Joyce's use of the song title 'Finnegan's Wake', for his novel?

17. When was Lawrence Sterne born?

18. For which book is Lawrence Sterne most famous?

18. What was the title of novelist Christopher Nolan's autobiography?

20. What is the forename of the Finnegan in *Finnegans Wake*?

Answers to Quiz 50

1. Bernard McLaverty

2. Clonmel, Co. Tipperary

3. Christopher Nolan

4. Myles na Gopaleen (he wrote novels under another pseudonym: see *Quiz 32*)

5. Old Gaelic poems and sagas

6. Brooklyn, NY, on 19th August 1930

7. Brian Moore

8. An honorary CBE (Commander, Order of the British Empire)

9. Landlords of Irish property who were not themselves resident in Ireland

10. *A Portrait of the Artist as a Young Man*

11. Gerald Griffin

12. James Plunkett

13. "To let down his country"

14. Derek Dougan

15. Walk through Ireland (*A Frenchman's Walk through Ireland 1796-7*)

16. The apostrophe was removed

17. November 1713

18. *Tristram Shandy*

19. *Under the Eye of the Clock*

20. Tim

1. What type of motor vehicle was produced in a Cork factory by 1917?

2. Which American manufacturer's vehicles were produced in Cork in 1917?

3. Who produced the Nobel 2000 in Co. Down?

4. In 1921 who were 'The Only Motor Car Manufacturers in Ireland'?

5. What nationality was JB Dunlop, father of the pneumatic tyre?

6. When was the Belleek Pottery founded?

7. Which Wexford export was enjoyed in England from 1171?

8. Where was Ireland's first aeroplane flown?

9. What is significant about W Collins and Co.?

10. Who founded Guinness' Brewery in 1759?

11. When did the transatlantic telegraph cable cease operation to Valentia Island?

12. What was unusual about the ship *Olympic*?

13. Name the paddle steamers which first crossed the Irish Sea in 1860?

14. In 1885 four Irish Sea-plying paddle steamers were joined by another. What was its name?

15. What was licensed in Tramore Bay in 1862?

16. As well as being eaten, what was seaweed once used as?

17. Which aptly named gentleman gained a license for oyster beds in Cork harbour, in the 1860s?

18. What underwater structure did *Olympic* collide with in 1918?

19. When did Ferguson Tractor Company merge with Massey to become Massey-Ferguson?

20. What links the Dublin businesses founded by Boland and Jacob, historically?

Answers to Quiz 51

1. Tractor

2. Henry Ford (whose grandfather was Irish)

3. Short Bros. & Harland Ltd.

4. Chambers Motors Ltd of Belfast

5. Scottish

6. 1857

7. Herring

8. Hillsborough, Co. Down, 31st December 1909

9. They produced bicycles and Dunlop's new tyres for Dunlop himself

10. Arthur Guinness

11. 1966

12. It rammed and sank a German U-boat in the First World War

13. Ulster, Munster, Leinster, Connaught

14. Ireland

15. Cultivation of oysters

16. Fertiliser

17. Ebenezer Pike

18. The U-boat U-103

19. 1958

20. Boland's Mill and Jacob's Biscuit Factory were both occupied during the Easter Rising

1. Which Irish actor appeared in the Roger Vadim film *Barbarella*, as the villainous Durand Durand?

2. Liam Neeson was Oscar-nominated for which 1993 film?

3. Stephen Boyd played opposite Raquel Welsh in which submarine drama?

4. Which film series prominently featured a Dunmurry-built DeLorean car?

5. At what speed did Dr Brown's DeLorean achieve time travel?

6. Which film maker produced *Man of Aran* in 1934?

7. Neil Jordan won which Oscar for his film *The Crying Game*?

8. In which year did George Bernard Shaw win an Academy Award?

9. Greer Garson won an Oscar in 1942 for her portrayal of which courageous character?

10. What is the character played by John Wayne in *The Quiet Man*?

11. Which Irish actor famously played opposite Charlton Heston in *Ben Hur*?

12. Which 1999 film by Alan Parker starred two non-Irish actors as the Irish parents of writer Frank McCourt?

13. Which film by the production team behind *Trainspotting* and *Shallow Grave* had a hit song from the northern Irish band Ash?

14. Colm Meaney play a harassed Dublin father in which Stephen Frears film?

15. Which film featured a horse called Tir na nÓg?

16. Bob Geldof starred as a rock musician in which Alan Parker film?

17. *Still Crazy*, a film about a British rock group's comeback, starred which Irish actor?

18. What is the character played by Victor McLaglen in *The Quiet Man*?

19. What is the character played by Maureen O'Hara in *The Quiet Man*?

20. How did 'Sean Thornton' make a living before his return to Ireland in *The Quiet Man*?

1. Milo O'Shea

2. *Schindler's List*, based on *Schindler's Ark*, by Thomas Kinealy

3. *Fantastic Voyage*

4. *Back To The Future*, Parts 1-3

5. 88 miles per hour

6. Robert Flaherty

7. Screenplay

8. 1938 (for his screen adaptation of *Pygmalion*, his own play)

9. *Mrs Miniver*

10. Sean Thornton

11. Stephen Boyd

12. *Angela's Ashes*

13. *A Life Less Ordinary*

14. *The Snapper*

15. *Into the West*

16. Pink Floyd's *The Wall*

17. Stephen Rea

18. Will Danaher ('Red' Will)

19. Mary Kate Danaher

20. A boxer

1. Where is Bully's Acre?

2. Where is Bullock?

3. St Canice of Kilkenny had his principal church at Aghaboe. In which present-day county could it be found?

4. Which county contains the village of Golden?

5. Knockfierna, the 'hill of truth' is found in which county?

6. What was the capital of the ancient Province of Ulster?

7. In which Youghal house were the first potatoes planted in Ireland?

8. What is the county town of Laois?

9. What is the county town of Antrim?

10. Where would you find WB Yeats' Nobel Prize?

11. Where is Geneva, once home to gold- and silversmiths?

12. In which county is the barony of Clankee?

13. What is Bully's Acre?

14. Where is the 'marble city'?

15. Moycullen, 'the plain of holly' is found in which county?

16. What was the capital of the ancient kingdom of Ossory?

17. What is the highest point in Ulster?

18. What is the county town of Limerick?

19. What is the county town of Clare?

20. Leitrim, Roscommon and Mayo share a border with which county?

1. Dublin's Royal Hospital at Kilmainham

2. Dalkey, Co. Dublin

3. Co. Laois

4. Co. Tipperary

5. Co. Limerick

6. Emain, 'the Navan', close to Armagh city

7. Myrtle Grove, Youghal

8. Portlaoise

9. Ballymena

10. In Sligo County Museum

11. Near Duncannon in Co. Wexford – in the 18th century, it was home to European gold- and silversmiths

12. Co. Cavan

13. Dublin's oldest cemetery

14. Kilkenny

15. Co. Galway

16. Kilkenny

17. Slieve Donard

18. Limerick

19. Ennis

20. Sligo

1. Why should O'Leary have been expected to sell his horse for a small price?

2. When did Wolfe Tone die?

3. When was Wolfe Tone born?

4. What were 'Carders' in the early-18th century?

5. Which Irish port suffered a blockade from 2nd May – 16th October 1649?

6. How did James Connolly die?

7. When did Ireland enter the newly-formed United Kingdom?

8. What was the name of Erskine Childers' gun-running yacht?

9. What gave the 'Carders' their name?

10. What took place on 12th January 1603 at the mouth of the Liffey?

11. What movement began in 1791?

12. Where did the notorious Irish soldier Colonel Blood die?

13. In 1170, who was King of Connaught and High King of Ireland?

14. What were 'inter Anglos' and 'inter Hibernicos'?

15. For what in Dublin were Thomas Burke, Edward Lovett Pearce and James Gandon responsible?

16. When was Ireland last officially termed 'The Free State'?

17. Which of the rebels in 1916 had been a British colonial official and knight?

18. In which Irish shipyard was *Titanic* built?

19. Which ship of the Spanish Armada foundered off Dunluce Castle in 1588?

20. What was Lord Haw-Haw's hated 'catch-phrase'?

1. A Penal Law restricted Catholics to owning horses worth less than £5

2. 19th November 1798

3. Dublin on 20th June 1763

4. An Irish secret society

5. Kinsale

6. Executed by firing squad 12th May 1916

7. 1st January 1801, under the Act of Union

8. *Asgard*

9. For their habit of scraping a steel tooth comb across a person's flesh as punishment

10. The first pleasure boat race in Ireland under rules

11. Transportation of Irish prisoners to Australia

12. Bowling Alley, Westminster

13. Ruari O'Connor

14. Norman-settled land, and 'wild Irish' land

15. Buildings in Georgian Dublin, as architects

16. 1937

17. Sir Roger Casement

18. Harland & Wolff, Belfast

19. *Girona*

20. 'Germany calling, Germany calling...'

1. What is 'Satharn'?

2. What does 'Meitheamh' mean?

3. What does 'Lúnasa' mean?

4. What does 'Deireadh Fómhair' mean?

5. Which Irish man's name is often confused with an English woman's name?

6. What does 'flannbhui' mean in Irish?

7. What does 'dearg' mean in Irish?

8. What are 'cruibíns'?

9. What is Bord na Mona?

10. What was An Claidheamh Soluis?

11. What is the meaning of 'banshee'?

12. What is 'observatory' in Irish?

13. What does Boa Island mean in Irish?

14. What does 'uisce beatha' mean?

15. Who or what is 'sheela-na-gig'?

16. What was 'Saorstát Éireann'?

17. To what use was Grianán of Aileach once put?

18. What does Waterford's Irish name 'Port Láirge' mean?

19. What does Waterville, Co. Kerry's Irish name, 'An Coireán' mean?

20. Who or what are 'na mBráithre Chriostai'?

1. Saturday

2. June

3. August

4. October

5. Enda, with Edna

6. Orange

7. Red

8. Pig's feet, seen by some as edible

9. The Irish Turf / Coal Board

10. *The Sword of Light*, a newspaper of the Gaelic League

11. Woman of the fairy (bean-sidhe)

12. Réadlann

13. 'Inis Badhbha', Island of the War Goddess

14. 'Water of Life'

15. An ancient female fertility symbol

16. Free State

17. The kings of Ulster once held court at this Donegal location

18. Large's Landing Place

19. The Small Weir

20. Christian Brothers

1. Which Irish groups has Christy Moore played in?

2. Which Irish singer is famous for his cardigans and rocking chair?

3. Where was Chris de Burgh born?

4. For which Stanley Kubrick film did The Chieftains provide music?

5. When did The Corrs release *Forgiven Not Forgotten*?

6. Barry Douglas is a famous Irish musician. What instrument does he play?

7. Who is well-acquainted with both 'Patricia the Stripper' and 'Lady in Red'?

8. With which Irish 'boy-band' did Ronan Keating come to notice?

9. When did the first Irish duo win Eurovision Song Contest for Ireland?

10. When was the Ash album *1977* released?

11. Which two television series with Christian names in the title featured Clannad's music?

12. Which Irish singer once 'co-managed' Westlife?

13. In which year did Dana win the Eurovision Song Contest?

14. Who sang 'Rock and Roll Kids', Ireland's winner in Eurovision Song Contest in 1994?

15. When was the 'Soldier's Song' written?

16. Which Irish song is also a James Joyce novel?

17. Which 'Scottish' group was founded by musicians born on the island of Ireland?

18. Which Irish musical group took its name from a famous United Irishman?

19. With which instrument was Derek Bell famously associated?

20. Where were the Clancy Brothers from?

1. Moving Hearts and Planxty

2. Val Doonican

3. Argentina, in 1948

4. *Barry Lyndon*

5. 1995

6. Piano

7. Chris de Burgh

8. Boyzone

9. 1994 – with 'Rock and Roll Kids'

10. 1996

11. *Robin of Sherwood, Harry's Game*

12. Ronan Keating

13. 1970

14. Paul Harrington and Charlie McGettigan

15. 1907

16. 'Finnegan's Wake' (*Finnegans Wake*)

17. Snow Patrol

18. The Wolfe Tones

19. The harp

20. Carrick-on-Suir, Co. Tipperary

1. Who said this in 1992? "There won't be a cow milked in Clare tonight".

2. Glenveagh Castle and estate comprise Ireland's first example of?

3. What was the theme to Byrne's *The Late Late Show*?

4. Who designed the videogame / cartoon character Earthworm Jim?

5. What were the Hearts of Oak and the Hearts of Steel?

6. What was the 'Ulster Custom'?

7. What is Irish Spurge?

8. What is the difference between a 'bobby' and a 'peeler'?

9. What is the link between 'bobbies' and 'peelers'?

10. What were Corry's Stars?

11. What opened in 1887 at Baltimore?

12. What name is shared by an 18th-century writer and a former world squash champion?

13. What was the 'True-Born Irishman' in 18th-century Ireland?

14. Who was described as "the Spanish onion in the Irish stew"?

15. Which Irish hero met with Queen Victoria in 1871 after a third 'Waterloo' victory?

16. What was notable about Master McGrath?

17. Which 'other' William and James, who share a surname if nothing else, are notorious, not for their battles, but for their words?

18. What is Pierce's Table?

19. What was 'Ireland's Saturday Night'?

20. What was a 'croppy'?

1. Marty Morrissey, commentator, on Kilkenny's defeat of Wexford in Croke Park

2. National Park

3. 'To Whom It Concerns'

4. Dave Perry, originally from Northern Ireland

5. 18th-century secret societies

6. A system of security for tenants, fair rent and tenure of land

7. A poisonous plant

8. A 'bobby' was a term for 19th-century English police, a 'peeler' was its Irish counterpart

9. Sir Robert Peel, founder and 'namesake' of both police forces

10. Sailing ships built by Harland & Wolff for a Mr Corry

11. The world's first 'Industrial Fishing School'

12. Jonah Barrington

13. A play written by Charles Macklin, *c.* 1760

14. Éamon de Valera

15. Master McGrath

16. The greyhound won the Waterloo Cup three times

17. William Joyce (Lord Haw-Haw), James Joyce

18. A cromlech on Luganquilla

19. A sports newspaper

20. An Irish person imitating the short hairstyle, manners and perhaps political views of a French Republican

1. When did Donegal win their first All-Ireland Senior football championship?

2. How many boxing medals did Ireland win in the 1984 Olympics?

3. Which Irishman won joint Bronze medal in boxing in 1956 Olympics?

4. Who was John Caldwell's joint Bronze medallist in 1956?

5. What might qualify as Ireland's 'first' real Olympics?

6. What was notable about the Gaelic Football championships in 1999?

7. When was the Irish Football Association formed?

8. The Irish Football Association was formed at which location, in which city?

9. What was Ireland's first football club?

10. In what year were Bohemians founded in Dublin?

11. What sport is played by Bohemians?

12. Which sport was ruled by the Irish Football Union, in November 1874?

13. What unusual article did DB Walkington wear while playing for Ireland in 1887?

14. How many players-a-side contested the 1887 All-Ireland Hurling final?

15. How many medals did Ireland win in 1928, its first Olympics as a Republic?

16. How many medals did Ireland win in the 1956 Olympics?

17. How many medals did Ireland win in the 1980 Olympics?

18. When did John Treacy win Silver in the Olympic Marathon?

19. In which event did Jamie Costin represent Ireland at 2000, 2004 and 2008 Olympics?

20. Which Irishman won a joint Bronze medal in boxing in 1980 Olympics?

1. 1992

2. One Bronze

3. John Caldwell

4. René Libeer of France

5. The first modern Olympics in 1896

6. New York competed for the first time

7. 18th November 1880

8. Queen's Hotel, Belfast

9. Cliftonville

10. 1890

11. Soccer

12. Rugby

13. A monocle

14. 21-a-side

15. One, but that was a Gold

16. Five, one Gold, one Silver, three Bronze

17. Two, one Silver, one Bronze

18. 1984

19. 50km Walk

20. Hugh Russell

1. Which mathematical physicist was born in Magheragall, Co. Antrim, in 1857?

2. Which post connects Sir Isaac Newton and Sir Joseph Larmor?

3. What was John Joly's main scientific interest?

4. Professor Thomas Romney Robinson invented which scientific instrument in 1843?

5. Where was the famous hydrographer Francis Beaufort born?

6. Which animal is called 'broc' in Irish?

7. What is *neotinea intacta*?

8. Which Irish dog is characterised by thick brown curly fur and a 'rat-like' tail?

9. Which Irish dog was bred to hunt deer?

10. Which Irish dog was bred to hunt a now-extinct Irish canine ancestor?

11. Which Irish dog is named for a county and a colour?

12. The *Skibbereen Eagle* challenged which 'double-headed bird of prey' in the 19th century?

13. What is Boyle's Law?

14. What was the name of the 19th-century telescope at Birr Castle?

15. In which university is the Guy Wilson Daffodil Garden?

16. To which Irishman do we owe the book *The Origin of Species*?

17. Against which skin complaint was Irish Spurge sometimes used?

18. Which measurement of windspeed is named after an Irishman?

19. Which bird gives its name to Mullary Cross in Co. Louth?

20. Who wrote 'Like crows attacking crow-black fields, they stretch'?

1. Sir Joseph Larmor

2. Lucasian Professor of Mathematics, Cambridge

3. The age of the Earth

4. Anemometer (windspeed gauge)

5. In his father's Church of Ireland rectory, Navan, in 1774

6. The badger

7. The Burren Orchid

8. Irish Water Spaniel

9. Deerhound

10. Irish Wolfhound

11. Kerry Blue

12. The newspaper once ran an editorial warning imperial Russia (emblem including a 'double-headed eagle') that it had its 'eye on them'

13. 'the volume of a fixed quantity of a gas at a constant temperature is inversely proportional to its pressure'

14. 'Leviathan'

15. University of Ulster, Coleraine

16. Francis Beaufort, who recommended that Charles Darwin be part of the *Beagle*'s voyage in the 1830s

17. Warts

18. The Beaufort Scale

19. The lark. The Irish name of 'Mullary Cross' is Mullach Lámhraighe; Lavrock's Height (lavrock or laverock is the lark)

20. Seamus Heaney (from 'At a Potato Digging')

1. Which son of a former Lord Mayor of Dublin was involved heavily in World War II?

2. What was the full name of Lady Wilde?

3. Who wrote 'Work is the curse of the drinking classes'?

4. Whose words did the subject of *question 3* paraphrase?

5. Which Irish family's crest features 'an arm couped at the shoulder, embowed ppr., vested gu., holding in hand a flag, sa., charged with a bee'?

6. What post did George Stoney hold?

7. When was the revolutionary printer John Dunlap (Dunlop) born?

8. What was Sean O'Casey's religion?

9. What was Ireland's population in 1911?

10. Which tragic figure is said to have given her name to Chapelizod, Dublin?

11. What does the suffix 'Óg' mean in a person's name?

12. Who was 'Humanity Dick'?

13. What does the Irish name 'Hickey' mean?

14. What does JM stand for in JM Synge?

15. Which Irish actor appeared in a double act with a horse in the film *The Quiet Man*?

16. Who founded the Peace People?

17. Which international honour were the two founders of the Peace People awarded?

18. Who founded St Enda's School, Dublin?

19. In what field was Rowel Friers most famous?

20. Who killed Strongbow?

1. General Sir Frederick 'Tim' Pile

2. Lady Jane Francesca Wilde

3. Oscar Wilde

4. Attributed to Karl Marx among others ('drink is the curse of the working classes')

5. Adams

6. Professor of Natural Philosophy

7. Born in 1747, he died in 1812

8. Protestant

9. 4.39 million according to census 2nd April 1911

10. Iseult (Tristram and Isolde)

11. 'Young' or Junior, as in Séan Óg

12. Richard Martin

13. Healer 'iceadh' in Irish

14. John Millington

15. Barry Fitzgerald

16. Mairead Corrigan and Betty Williams

17. 1977 Nobel Prize for Peace

18. Padraig Pearse

19. As a humourist / cartoonist and caricaturist

20. According to the Four Masters, 'he saw, he thought, St Brigid in the act of killing him'. He actually died of an infection in 1176.

1. Through which county does the river Derry flow?
2. Where was future President Erskine Childers born?
3. Why is 'Joyce's Country' in Co. Galway so-called?
4. Where is Kilmogue Dolmen?
5. In which city was de Valera born?
6. In which county is Birr Castle?
7. What are the subterranean limestone caves found near Florencecourt, Co. Fermanagh picturesquely called?
8. What is the county town of Kerry?
9. What is the county town of Kilkenny?
10. What is the county town of Dublin?
11. Where was Ernest Shackleton born?
12. Where was Ernest Shackleton buried?
13. Where is the Nore Valley?
14. In which county is Cape Clear?
15. What is the largest fresh water expanse in the British Isles?
16. In which county is Muckish Mountain?
17. Which province lends its name to a cloth overcoat?
18. Where is the Shackleton crater located?
19. What is the county town of Cork?
20. What is the county town of Westmeath?

1. Carlow

2. London, 11th December 1905

3. After 13th-century Welsh settlers, of the family Joyce

4. Co. Waterford

5. New York

6. Co. Offaly

7. Marble Arch Caves

8. Tralee

9. Kilkenny

10. Dublin

11. Ballytore, Co. Kildare in 1874

12. South Georgia, an island in the South Atlantic

13. Kilkenny

14. Cork

15. Lough Neagh

16. Donegal

17. Ulster

18. In the south polar region of the Moon

19. Cork

20. Mullingar

1. Which seat of government did Robert Emmet attack?

2. How many famines had 19th-century Ireland experienced before the Great Famine?

3. In 1874, who was the High Sheriff of Wicklow?

4. What was built on Belfast's Falls Road in 1829?

5. Which ancient kingdom spanned Ireland and Scotland?

6. In what year was Trinity College, Dublin, founded?

7. Why was Cobh renamed Queenstown?

8. How many ships were in the French fleet with Wolfe Tone in 1796?

9. How many of the 1796 French fleet's ships landed in Ireland?

10. Which town in Derry is the birth-place of the man who announced the American Declaration of Independence?

11. What did the 1366 Statutes of Kilkenny generally prohibit?

12. Who was the first Earl of Ranelagh?

13. When was Ireland first termed 'The Free State'?

14. A memorial to the Irish dead of which war was placed in Dublin's Methodist Centenary Church?

15. What was the original name of the area which is now Phoenix Park?

16. What do the initials IRB stand for?

17. What do the initials IRA stand for?

18. What do the initials ICA stand for?

19. On which common date were the IRB and Fenian Brotherhood founded?

20. Which country did a group calling itself the 'Irish Republican Army' enter unlawfully in summer 1866?

1. Dublin Castle, as part of a small 'rebellion'

2. Six

3. Charles Stewart Parnell

4. Lunatic asylum

5. Dal Riada

6. 1592

7. To mark the visit of King George VI and his Queen

8. Forty-three

9. None

10. Maghera, 1729

11. The mixing of English colonists and Irish people, their language and law

12. Richard Jones

13. 1922

14. First World War

15. Fionn uisg – 'clear stream'

16. Irish Republican Brotherhood

17. Irish Republican Army

18. Irish Citizen Army

19. 17th March 1858

20. Canada, occupying parts of the town of Port Erie

1. In which language did write Eileen O'Leary 'The Lament for Art O'Leary"?

2. Who owned the Co. Mayo estates managed by the infamous Charles Cunningham Boycott?

3. In the world of 19th-century fishing, who was 'Ephemera'?

4. Which group was first accepted into Trinity College Dublin from 1793?

5. As what is Father Theobald Mathew remembered?

6. Which Irish businessman imported tea directly from China to Dublin in 1835?

7. Who first prepared 'Irish coffee'?

8. By whose reckoning was a journey from Galway–St John's, Newfoundland "the shortest route between this country and America"?

9. On whose life was the film *The General* based?

10. What in Ireland is 'The Holy Land'?

11. Who said "If I knew who Godot was, I would have said so"?

12. When was Ireland's first 'test-tube baby' born?

13. When was the third Nobel Peace Prize awarded to Irish people?

14. In which field was William Dargan (1799-1867), famous?

15. Who founded the Stud Farm which became the National Stud?

16. Who were the 'Four Masters'?

17. Which Irishman was a pioneer of the agricultural tractor?

18. Who was curate at Boolavogue in April 1798, during the Rising?

19. Who was the First Earl of Athlone?

20. Which Irish philosopher had a Californian city named after him in 1866, 113 years after his death?

1. Irish

2. Earl of Erne

3. Edward Fitzgibbon of Limerick, born 1803

4. Catholic students

5. Temperance campaigner

6. Samuel Bewley

7. Joe Sheridan, in 1943

8. Galway Royal Mail line

9. Martin Cahill

10. An area in Belfast made up of Jerusalem Street, Palestine Street and Damascus Street

11. Samuel Beckett

12. 15th January 1986

13. December 1998

14. Irish railways

15. Lord Wavertree

16. Michael O'Clery, Farfasa O'Mulchrony, Peregrine O'Clery and Peregrine O'Dingenan, who compiled much ancient Irish history

17. Harry Ferguson

18. Father John Murphy

19. Godard van Reede, born 1644

20. George Berkeley

1. Why was Dun Laoghaire re-named 'Kingstown'?

2. Tambour and run are types of which decorative work?

3. What does the Latin phrase 'hiberniores hibernis ipsos' mean?

4. Which word can be both an accent and a shoe?

5. On which English college was Trinity College Dublin based?

6. What happened to the 'Empress of Ireland' in 1914?

7. What novel enterprise was set up in Oughterard in 1852?

8. In which industrial processes was 'kelp' principally used?

9. What property of 'kelp' made it very useful in industrial processes?

10. What were the 'Blueshirts'?

11. What was the 'Sixth of George I'?

12. What was 'Cumann na nGaedhael'?

13. What was 'an tSlighe Mhór'?

14. What was the Severe Pine Tree Buttress?

15. What became illegal in Ireland on 28th February 1935?

16. On which date did Dublin catch up with London?

17. Arklow in Co. Wicklow was the first place in Ireland to have which life-saving service?

18. Which organisation participated in a demonstration sport in the fourth modern Olympics?

19. What can be found at 53° 00′ N, 8° 00′ W?

20. What are the Gobbins?

1. Following the visit of King George VI in 1821

2. Limerick lace

3. 'More Irish than the Irish'

4. Brogue

5. Trinity College, Cambridge

6. A Canadian Pacific liner, it sank after a collision in the St Lawrence seaway with the deaths of over 1000 people

7. The first commercial salmon fishery

8. In the manufacture of soap and glass

9. It was a good source of carbonate of soda

10. An Irish fascist organisation

11. A law stating that the English parliament could pass laws which were binding in Ireland

12. A political movement

13. The ancient Great Road, linking Dublin with the west coast

14. A climbing route on Luggala, Co. Wicklow

15. Sale and importation of contraceptives

16. 23rd August 1916, with the introduction of Greenwich Mean Time (GMT)

17. A lifeboat station

18. Irish Bicycle Polo Association

19. Ireland (latitude and longitude, map co-ordinates)

20. *c.* 250ft basalt cliffs near Islandmagee, Co. Antrim

1. Who was joint Bronze medallist with boxer Hugh Russell in 1980?

2. Which honour did boxer Wayne McCullough win in Barcelona?

3. Who beat Wayne McCullough to win Olympic Gold in 1992?

4. At which boxing weight did Wayne McCullough compete?

5. Who was the first non-native to manage Ireland's international soccer team?

6. George Best is famous as a player for which football club?

7. Which world-famous rugby side did Munster beat in 1978?

8. When was the Irish Ladies' Hockey Union founded?

9. About which international rally event did Paddy Hopkirk write a book
    entitled *The Longest Drive of All*?

10. The Irish Football Union and which other formed the Irish Rugby
    Football Union?

11. When was the Irish Rugby Football union formed?

12. Why would DB Walkington, rugby player, never be far from a quiz?

13. Ireland beat a world-class side on 2nd July 1969. In which sport?

14. Which team did Ireland defeat on 2nd July 1969, and in which Irish
    town did the match take place?

15. Paddy Barnes and Darren Sutherland won Bronze medals in which
    boxing divisions in the 2008 Olympics?

16. Which sport first took hold in Ireland in Cork during 1880s?

17. When was the first fully-documented match of women's cricket in Ireland?

18. Dalkey Quarry was an important development site in which sport?

19. Between which teams was the first Hockey international played?

20. Who won the first Hockey international, and where was this match played?

1. Hungary's Janos Varadi

2. Olympic Silver

3. Jose Casamayor of Cuba

4. Bantamweight

5. Jack Charlton

6. Manchester United

7. New Zealand's All Blacks

8. 1894

9. The London-Sydney marathon

10. Northern Football Union

11. February 1879

12. 'Quiz' is another, obsolete name for a monocle, which Walkington famously wore even while playing!

13. Cricket

14. The West Indies, at Sion Mills, Co. Derry

15. Light flyweight and middleweight

16. Women's cricket

17. 1936

18. Rock climbing

19. Wales and Ireland

20. Ireland won by 3-0 at Rhyl in Wales

1. Which playwright is famous for *Philadelphia Here I Come*?

2. Who wrote the play *The Playboy of the Western World*?

3. Where was actor Liam Neeson born?

4. Which Séan O'Casey character is the Captain's sidekick?

5. Which O'Casey play takes its title from a worker's flag?

6. Name the main female character in Sean O'Casey's play *Juno and the Paycock*.

7. Which Irish dramatist was awarded the Nobel Prize in 1925?

8. What was the original title of Dublin's Abbey Theatre?

9. What is a 'paycock', as in *Juno and the Paycock*?

10. Where was Samuel Beckett's *Waiting for Godot* first performed?

11. Where was actor Cyril Cusack born?

12. Who founded Dublin's Abbey Theatre?

13. Which 1970s American situation comedy set in the 1950s shares its title with a 1960 Samuel Beckett play?

14. Who wrote *Krapp's Last Tape*?

15. Which Irish playwright wrote *The Field*?

16. The great actress Siobhan McKenna was best known for which role in JM Synge's *Playboy of the Western World*?

17. What is the name of the main male character in Sean O'Casey's *Juno and the Paycock*?

18. Which early Irish President had a play staged in Dublin's Gaiety Theatre?

19. Who starred alongside Michael Flatley in the original 'Riverdance'?

20. Which play caused riots in Dublin, 1907?

1. Brian Friel

2. JM Synge

3. Ballymena, Co. Antrim

4. Joxer Daley in *Juno and the Paycock*

5. *The Plough and the Stars* (The Starry Plough)

6. Juno Boyle

7. George Bernard Shaw

8. Irish National Theatre

9. An Irish pronunciation of the word 'peacock'

10. Paris, France

11. Durban, South Africa, 26th November 1910

12. Lady Gregory, Edward Martyn, George Moore

13. *Happy Days*

14. Samuel Beckett

15. John B Keane

16. Pegeen Mike

17. 'Captain' Jack Boyle

18. Douglas Hyde (*Casadh an tSúgain*) 1901

19. Jean Butler

20. *Playboy of the Western World*

1. Tyrone, Fermanagh and Leitrim share a border with which county?

2. Magilligan Point and Greencastle are found to the north of which body of water?

3. Between which towns did Charles Bianconi's 19th-century stage network first operate?

4. Where is Crookhaven?

5. Which Kildare town is also a part of the leg?

6. Which river flows into Dublin Bay at Clontarf?

7. In which county is Naas, the most ancient residence of the kings of Leinster?

8. Two counties have a town called Nurney. Name them.

9. Which county contains Slievenamon, 'mountain of the women'?

10. What separates Ireland from Wales?

11. In which county is Ardagh, famous for the golden chalice?

12. What was the capital of the ancient Province of Connacht?

13. What is the county town of Galway?

14. What is the county town of Meath?

15. In which county are the Curlew Mountains?

16. Which is the O'Moore County?

17. What is Donegal's Knockalla Mountain also known as?

18. On which hill did Ireland's fair maids vie for the honour of being Finn MacCool's wife?

19. Tory Island is found off the coast of which county?

20. Wood of O lies near a midlands town. Name it, and its county.

1. Donegal

2. Lough Foyle

3. Cahir and Clonmel

4. At the tip of Toormore Bay, Co. Cork

5. Athy

6. The Tolka

7. Co. Kildare

8. Co. Carlow, Co. Kildare

9. Co. Tipperary

10. St George's Channel, and the Irish Sea

11. Longford

12. Cruachain, Rathcrogan, Co. Roscommon

13. Galway

14. Trim

15. Sligo

16. Laois

17. Devil's Backbone

18. Slievenamon, Co. Tipperary

19. Co. Donegal

20. Tullamore, Co. Offaly

1. What did RIC stand for?

2. What did the RIC become in the 1920s?

3. Which northern civic building opened on 1st August 1906?

4. What was the Irish police force called after 1922?

5. What did GNR stand for in 19th-century Ireland?

6. When was Trinity College, Dublin founded?

7. When was University College Dublin founded?

8. Who introduced coinage into Ireland?

9. When was Queenstown renamed?

10. What was the name of the British ship captured by John Barry?

11. What did the *Times* call O'Connell's mass gatherings?

12. From what were women exempted by the Synod of Tara, 697AD?

13. Scarva in Co. Down holds what on 13th July each year?

14. Where was the Irish terminal of the Atlantic cable?

15. What was the purpose of the Atlantic cable, which was completed in 1866?

16. Of which town was Sir Walter Raleigh warden from 1588-89?

17. When was Crumlin Road Gaol completed?

18. When was the University of Cork founded?

19. Who said in 1896 "I am resolved to take whatever course is best for Ireland"?

20. Who said that "The repeal of the External Relations Act will take the gun out of Irish politics"?

1. Royal Irish Constabulary

2. Royal Ulster Constabulary

3. Belfast City Hall

4. Garda Síochána

5. Great Northern Railway

6. 1591

7. 1908

8. Sitric, Norse King of Dublin

9. 1920

10. The *Edward*

11. Monster meetings

12. Fighting in battle

13. A 'sham fight' commemorating the Battle of the Boyne 1690

14. Valentia Island

15. To enable telegraphic communication between Europe and America

16. Youghal

17. 1846

18. 1908

19. Edward Carson

20. John A Costello, on 14th November 1948

1. Which English designer and architect planned the gardens at Heywood?
2. Which Irish actress played a villain opposite both 'Indiana Jones' and 'James Bond'?
3. Liam Neeson married which English actress in 1994?
4. Which Irish naval explorer was the first to travel the North West Passage?
5. Which famous Irishman was nephew to Eileen O'Leary?
6. What was the real name of Irish writer Frank O'Connor?
7. Who was offered the rule of Ireland in 1263?
8. Who was the first woman to steam across the Atlantic?
9. Who described Sir William Ferguson as "some ancient sea-king sitting among the inland wheat and poppies"?
10. Who was known as the 'Long Fellow'?
11. Who wrote "Ireland without her people is nothing to me"?
12. Who said that Dublin Castle was "the best machine... for governing a country against its will"?
13. Who was Molly Maguire?
14. What does the name 'Colmcille' mean?
15. Who was known as St Richard of Dundalk?
16. What is the Irish meaning of the name 'Aherne' or 'Ahern'?
17. The 'Aherne' family crest shows three animals – what are they?
18. Which important equestrian figure once lived in Grangemellon Castle near Levitstown Crossroads, Co. Kildare?
19. Who founded the RIC in 1814?
20. When did JM Synge die?

1. Sir Edward Lutyens

2. Alison Doody

3. Natasha Richardson

4. Sir Robert John Le Mesurier McClure

5. Daniel O'Connell

6. Michael O'Donovan

7. King Haakon IV

8. Miss Linch, as stewardess on board the *Sirius*, April 1838

9. WB Yeats

10. Éamon de Valera

11. James Connolly, on 7th July 1900

12. John Morley, Liberal MP, on 12th May 1902

13. An Irish widow involved in protests against landlords in the 1840s

14. 'Dove of the Church'

15. Richard Fitzralph, Archbishop of Armagh

16. 'Lord of the horses'

17. Herons

18. Colonel St Leger, namesake of the famous classic horse race

19. Sir Robert Peel

20. 24th March 1909

1. Which type of race takes place near Cape Clear?
2. What are the North and South Slobs in Wexford?
3. "'I do not know', said the man, 'what the custom of the English may be, but it is the custom of the Irish to hate villains.'" From which 19th-century novel is this quote taken?
4. What is a 'turlough'?
5. Where was the first 'Irish coffee' produced?
6. What is a coracle?
7. Who were the 'Molly Maguires'?
8. What does RDS stand for?
9. What is boxty?
10. How many men play on a hurling side?
11. What were the 'Wild Geese'?
12. What is a 'shillelagh' commonly thought to be?
13. Where does the term 'shillelagh' come from?
14. In 2004, Dr Clare O'Leary became the first Irish woman to reach which peak of human achievement?
15. Which distinction did Ireland share with Belarus before the 2000 Olympics?
16. What was a 'Teltown marriage'?
17. What spends six months of every year on Wexford Harbour's North Slob?
18. When was the collared dove introduced to Ireland?
19. What are Kilkenny Cats?
20. What do the 'Walls of Limerick' and 'The Bridge of Athlone' have in common, aside from their construction?

1. Fastnet Yacht Race

2. Reclaimed alluvial land

3. *Frankenstein*, by Mary Shelley, 1818

4. A limestone lake, which dries in summer, to appear again after heavy rainfall

5. Shannon Airport

6. An ancient hide covered, cylindrical boat

7. A workers' movement in 19th-century Pennsylvania, with origins in Ireland

8. Royal Dublin Society

9. An Irish potato recipe

10. Fifteen

11. Irish soldiers serving in the Irish Brigade of the French army in the 1690s

12. A walking stick, or sometimes a 'cudgel', made from blackthorn wood

13. The woods around Shillelagh in Co. Wicklow were a great source of such wood

14. She climbed Mount Everest

15. Equal 44th in Olympic medal ranking

16. A marriage which held together for "only a year and a day"

17. Half of the world's population of Greenland white-fronted geese (6000)

18. 1959

19. Cats so fierce that, when they fought, there was nothing left of them but tails – hence 'they fought like Kilkenny cats'.

20. They are Irish dances

1. Ken Egan won which medal in the light heavyweight division in the 2008 Olympics?

2. Phil Casey of Mountrath was the first world champion in which sport, in 1889?

3. What was the GAA invasion of USA in 1886?

4. What distance did Ireland's first Gordon-Bennett race cover?

5. When did Ireland's first Gordon-Bennett race take place?

6. Which event was the subject of sports' first radio commentary?

7. When was the first Irish rugby international?

8. When did Ireland first win rugby's 'Triple Crown'?

9. The 1896 Irish rugby side touring South Africa went on to win more than sporting honours in the country. What happened?

10. Which Irish rugby player was imprisoned over the disappearance of an Argentinian flag in 1980?

11. What did Ireland win in 1932, for the first time in 33 years?

12. Which Irish rugby international also had Olympic importance?

13. Which rugby player said "I hate small men"?

14. When did Willie John McBride score his first international try?

15. When was the McCarthy Cup first presented in gaelic games?

16. After whom is the McCarthy Cup named?

17. For which English football team have Jennings, O'Leary and Stapleton played?

18. Which Irish soccer internationals of the same name ended their careers 41 years apart?

19. Who was the first Irish woman to take part in an Olympic swimming final?

20. What sort of race was Gordon-Bennett?

1. Silver medal
2. Handball
3. GAA teams visited America en masse
4. 328 miles
5. 1903
6. A yacht race off Kingstown in 1898
7. 15th February 1875
8. 1894
9. Two of the players went on to win the Victoria Cross during the Boer War (1899-1902)
10. Willie Anderson
11. Triple Crown
12. Joe Comiskey, who was doctor to the Irish Olympic squad
13. Willie John McBride
14. In his final home international
15. 1921
16. Liam McCarthy, once President of the Irish Athletic Association
17. Arsenal
18. Jimmy Dunne, 1930, 1971
19. Michelle Smith
20. An automobile race

1. Richard Harris starred in which famous rugby film?

2. For which Irish film did Brenda Fricker win an Academy Award?

3. What nationality are the male and female leads in Alan Parker's *Angela's Ashes*?

4. Which 'Prime Suspect' did John Lynch star alongside in *Cal*?

5. Which Irish folk hero did Liam Neeson play in a film by Neil Jordan?

6. Which soccer superstar is profiled in the film *Best*?

7. For which 'non-*Ocean's*' Steven Soderburgh film did David Holmes provide the soundtrack?

8. Which computer-animated film used the Thin Lizzy song 'The Boys are Back in Town'?

9. Which film starring Samuel L Jackson and Geena Davis features an Irish water spaniel?

10. Complete the title of a Peter O'Toole film – *My Favourite...*?

11. How many times had Peter O'Toole been nominated for an Academy Award, up to 2008?

12. How many Academy Awards did Peter O'Toole win, up to 2008?

13. Which film by the Coen brothers starred Gabriel Byrne?

14. Tom Berenger co-starred with which Irish actor in *The Field*?

15. Who directed the film *Best*?

16. Which Irish actor co-wrote *Best* with Mary McGuckian?

17. What was the title of the film in which Liam Neeson portrayed Michael Collins?

18. Which Irish-born actor links the Antichrist and dinosaurs?

19. Which Oscar Wilde-themed film starred both Brenda Fricker and Tara Fitzgerald?

20. What is Hollywood's most famous 'donnybrook'?

1. *This Sporting Life*

2. *My Left Foot*

3. Scottish

4. Helen Mirren

5. Michael Collins

6. George Best

7. *Out of Sight*

8. *Toy Story*

9. *The Long Kiss Goodnight*

10. '*Year*'

11. Eight times

12. None

13. *Miller's Crossing*

14. Richard Harris

15. Mary McGuckian

16. John Lynch

17. Michael Collins

18. Sam Neill, who starred in *Jurassic Park* and *Omen III–The Final Conflict*

19. *A Man of No Importance*

20. Between Victor McLaglen and John Wayne in *The Quiet Man*

1. Where is Boolavogue?
2. Which Irish county was divided into North and South Ridings?
3. In which city was JB Dunlop born?
4. What is the main function of Silent Valley in Co. Down?
5. What is the county town of Kildare?
6. What is the county town of Donegal?
7. What is Northern Ireland's smallest county?
8. What are Gowlaun, Twins and Rathbaum?
9. What is Feohanagh, Co. Limerick's 'Scottish' connection?
10. Where are the Twelve Bens?
11. What is the origin of the name Draperstown?
12. The hill of Knockninny is found in which northern county?
13. Desertserges, or 'Saerghus's hermitage', can be found in which
    southern county?
14. Where was the First Earl of Athlone born?
15. What number of Aran Islands are there?
16. When did rail travel begin from Belfast to Dublin?
17. The Spelga Pass links which towns?
18. Where is the Yellow Ford?
19. How were six new counties created in 1608?
20. Where would you find Two Rock Mountain and Three Rock Mountain?

1. Co. Wexford

2. Tipperary

3. Edinburgh

4. As a reservoir, and source of water for Belfast

5. Naas

6. Lifford

7. Armagh

8. Spas or springs at Lisdoonvarna, Co. Clare

9. It once meant 'place of the thistles' (a Scottish emblem)

10. Connemara

11. It was established by the London Company of Drapers during the Ulster Plantation

12. Co. Fermanagh

13. Co. Cork

14. Utrecht, Netherlands

15. Three

16. 1853

17. Kilkeel and Hilltown, Co. Down

18. On the River Blackwater

19. The lands were confiscated from those nobles who left Ireland in what became known as the Flight of the Earls

20. Kilternan, Co. Dublin

1. Which event was Jim Larkin most famous for opposing?

2. Who were attacked in Limerick in 1904?

3. What was the former name of Dublin's O'Connell Street?

4. Which British naval hero once had a monument on Dublin's O'Connell Street?

5. When did the first flight take place from Dublin Airport?

6. When was Dublin's O'Connell Bridge built?

7. What was O'Connell Bridge originally called?

8. When was O'Connell Bridge renamed?

9. When did Ernest Shackleton first visit the Antarctic?

10. How near the South Pole did Shackleton get in 1907?

11. When did Molly Malone die?

12. What is the term attached to 30th January 1972?

13. When was building of the Royal Belfast Academical Institution completed?

14. Which event coincided with the passing of Ireland's External Relations Act, 11th December 1936?

15. Name the writer of the following account of events leading up to the Dublin Lockout of September 1913: "People are thrown into prison for making the most peaceful speeches. The city is like an armed camp."

16. WB Yeats dealt with the Dublin Lockout in which famous poem?

17. Which American-born son of an Irishman infamously broadcast Nazi propaganda during World War Two?

18. By which title was the infamous Nazi propagandist and radio 'star' more commonly known?

19. What was unusual about the post-war fate of William Joyce?

20. Who commanded the Jacobite and Williamite forces at Aughrim?

1. The Dublin Lockout of August 1913

2. The city's Jewish community

3. Upper Sackville Street

4. Horatio Nelson

5. 1940

6. Between 1794-98

7. Carlisle Bridge

8. In 1882

9. 1902

10. Within 97 miles

11. 1734

12. 'Bloody Sunday'

13. 1814

14. The abdication of King Edward VIII

15. Vladimir Illyich Lenin

16. 'September 1913'

17. William Joyce April 24, 1906, New York, NY, USA

18. 'Lord Haw-Haw'

19. William Joyce was executed as a traitor although he was not British, but American-born

20. Generals St Ruth and Ginkel

1. Where did the word 'navvie' originate?

2. Which literary, radio, comic strip and film character has been played by an Englishman, Scotsman, Australian, and until 2002, by an Irishman?

3. What is 'The Point'?

4. What is fadge?

5. Who wrote 'The Famine knocked the heart out of the Irish language'?

6. What is notable about the South Pole Inn in Annascaul, Co. Kerry?

7. Which college educated both Jonathan Swift and Oliver Goldsmith?

8. Little Skellig island has Ireland's largest concentration of which animal?

9. What is Great Saltee?

10. Of what would an Irish Tory once have been accused?

11. What is a Tory today?

12. What were the Four Masters responsible for?

13. Who was the first Lord Mayor of Dublin?

14. What was a pitch-cap?

15. What was entitled 'LIBERTY, EQUALITY, FRATERNITY, UNION!'?

16. When was Dun Laoghaire re-named 'Kingstown'?

17. At 270m long and 28m high, what in 1912 was the world's largest man-made, mobile object?

18. What is Lisdoonvarna famous for?

19. What does ISPCA stand for?

20. Name the starting point of the first east-to-west solo powered Atlantic flight.

1. The labourers who dug 'navigation channels' on English canals in the 18th century

2. James Bond

3. A large concert venue in Dublin

4. Another name for Irish potato bread

5. Douglas Hyde, noted Gaelic scholar

6. It was run by Tom Crean, Antarctic explorer

7. Trinity College, Dublin

8. Gannet, the seabird

9. An offshore island important for nesting seabirds

10. Theft and villainy – a 'tory' was a thief, at least until the 16th century

11. A member of the British Conservative Party – a name adopted in the 18th century

12. A collection of Irish literature in the 17th century, such as *The Annals*

13. Richard Muton

14. A method of torture, involving burning molten tar

15. A French proclamation of 1798, issued after their landing in Mayo

16. After 1821

17. The liner *Titanic*

18. Its Bachelors' Festival

19. Irish Society for the Prevention of Cruelty to Animals

20. The Velvet Strand, Co. Dublin, by James Allan Mollison in a Puss Moth

1. Who wrote of Countess Markiewicz that she was 'a haggard woman returned'?

2. What did Joseph Plunkett's father do in 1917, recalling the actions of Constance Markiewicz?

3. Which American award did Irishman Glen Hansard and Czech woman Markéta Irglová receive in 2008?

4. Traditionally, when is the last day of the Irish summer?

5. Which of the founders of the *Titanic*'s shipyard lived to see the ship?

6. What are the full names of Harland and Wolff?

7. When did Edward Harland die?

8. When did Gustav Wolff die?

9. Which non-royal Irish family included a 'Prince' among them?

10. After whom was Croke Park named?

11. Who founded the Royal Canadian Mounted Police?

12. Who travelled under the pseudonym 'Sebastian Melmoth'?

13. What was Ireland's population in 1991?

14. Who was 'Wolfe Tone MacGowan'?

15. What was Éamon de Valera's given name?

16. To which group of languages does Irish belong?

17. What is Ireland's national airline?

18. Which heraldic crest is described 'issuing out of a cloud, a dexter arm, embowed brandishing a sword all propr.'?

19. What is the Irish motto of Baron O'Neill, of Shane's Castle, Antrim?

20. What is the English translation of Baron O'Neill's motto?

1. C Day-Lewis

2. He won a seat in the House of Commons, but did not take his seat (North Roscommon)

3. The Academy Award for 'Best Original Song' in the Irish film *Once*

4. Last Sunday in July

5. Wolff

6. Edward Harland and Gustav Wolff

7. 1895

8. 1913

9. The MacDermots

10. Archbishop Thomas Croke

11. George French, from Roscommon, in 1873

12. Oscar Wilde

13. 3.53 million according to census 21st April 1991

14. Jack B Yeats, who wrote poetry under this pseudonym

15. Edward De Valera

16. Goidelic

17. Aer Lingus

18. O'Brien, Earl of Thomond

19. 'Lamh dearg Eirin'

20. The Red Hand to Victory

1. When did Roscommon win their first All Ireland Senior Final?

2. When did the first Northern Ireland team win the Sam Maguire Cup?

3. Which team won the Sam Maguire Cup in 1960?

4. How many consecutive handball titles did Michael 'Duxie' Walsh win up to 1993?

5. Which sports did Wembley Stadium first host in May 1958?

6. Which Irish teams played in two matches at Wembley in 1958?

7. Which GAA county has its home ground at Ruislip?

8. Charles Stewart Parnell was once a steward at which Irish coastal race meeting?

9. Who wrote *My Road to Victory*, published in 1987?

10. Which sport used to include scores of 'Horsemen', 'Tally' and 'Look sharp'?

11. Which sport was United Irishman Michael Boylan, of Blakestown, Ardee, playing when he was arrested?

12. When was Ireland's first Olympic Games?

13. Where is the Irish 2000 Guineas run?

14. What do John Watson's first and last season in Formula One have in common?

15. Which sport was played by JJ Bowles?

16. The Irish rugby team of 1887 fielded the son of which gothic novelist?

17. What age was the racehorse Shergar when he was kidnapped?

18. Which English classic race did Shergar win twice?

19. For which country did Irish emigrant Patrick J Ryan win Gold in 1920 Olympics?

20. In which event did Patrick J Ryan win Olympic Gold?

Answers to Quiz 77

1. 1943

2. 1960

3. Down

4. Nine

5. Gaelic football and hurling

6. Galway and Derry, Kilkenny and Clare

7. London GAA

8. Laytown

9. Stephen Roche

10. Handball

11. Handball

12. 1924

13. The Curragh

14. He failed to gain any points

15. Handball

16. Victor Le Fanu, son of Sheridan

17. Five years of age

18. The Derby

19. USA

20. Hammer-throw

1. What is the county town of Offaly?

2. Kerry, Limerick, Tipperary and Waterford share a border with which county?

3. Which county in Leinster is the only one without a coastline?

4. Where is Fastnet Rock?

5. Where is Bonamargy Abbey?

6. The Cooley peninsula is situated in which county?

7. In which county would you find the Cliffs of Moher?

8. Which scientific building can be seen on Armagh's College Hill?

9. Where was Trinity College, Dublin founded?

10. Where was the mariner John Barry born?

11. Where was the publisher of America's first daily newspaper born?

12. What is the county town of Wicklow?

13. What is the better-known name of Tandragee Castle?

14. In which county does the River Boyne begin?

15. Under which city does the River Farset flow?

16. Which river flows through Cork city?

17. What does Cavan mean in Irish?

18. What can be found at Lissyviggeen?

19. In which county did the kings of Ulster once hold court?

20. Which ports were served by the 'province' steamers?

Answers to Quiz 78

1. Tullamore

2. Cork

3. Tipperary

4. 4 miles south-west of Cape Clear, Co. Cork

5. Ballycastle, Co. Antrim

6. Co. Louth

7. Co. Clare

8. The Armagh Observatory

9. In the grounds of the former monastery of All Hallows

10. Bally Sampson, 1745

11. John Dunlop, born in Strabane, Co. Down

12. Wicklow

13. Tayto Castle

14. Co. Kildare

15. Belfast

16. The River Lee

17. Hollow place

18. An ancient stone circle

19. Donegal

20. Kingstown and Holyhead in Wales

1. On what date did the IRA announce in Dublin that it had ended the terrorist campaign which it had carried out against Northern Ireland since December 1956?

2. What was the name given to the Celtic 'senate'?

3. When was the first full Irish Constitution enacted?

4. Éamon de Valera was President of the Council of which forerunner to the United Nations, in September 1932?

5. On what date did Eire withdraw from the British Commonwealth?

6. When was the first Northern Ireland parliament opened?

7. Éamon de Valera, as head of state, offered controversial condolence at the death of which leader?

8. When did Liam T Cosgrave die?

9. When did President John F Kennedy visit Ireland?

10. Which council did Ireland join on 1st January 1960?

11. When was Éamon de Valera elected President of Ireland?

12. When did Ireland join the United Nations?

13. On what date was the Garda Síochána established in law?

14. When was the 'Irish Free State' admitted to the League of Nations?

15. When were the first Free State postage stamps issued?

16. Who said "from the graves of patriot men and women spring living nations"?

17. Which country declared support for Irish independence in November 1914?

18. Which post did Irish scientist George Stokes hold in common with Sir Joseph Larmor?

19. Who was the 19th-century 'uncrowned King of Ireland'?

20. When was Brian Merriman born?

1. 26th February 1962

2. Aireacht

3. 29th December 1937

4. The League of Nations

5. 18th April 1949

6. 22nd June 1921

7. Adolf Hitler, April 1945

8. 16th November 1965

9. 26th June 1963

10. United Nations Security Council

11. 17th June 1959

12. 14th December 1955

13. 8th August 1923

14. 10th September 1923

15. 17th February 1922

16. Parick Pearse

17. Germany

18. Lucasian Professor of Mathematics, Cambridge University

19. Charles Stewart Parnell

20. 1747

1. Which Co. Carlow house brings to mind a notorious American music festival?

2. What is the female equivalent of the sport of hurling?

3. What was *cervus megaseros*?

4. Who or what is known as the 'Queen of the Nine Glens'?

5. Who was Danu?

6. Where did the term 'boycott' originate?

7. What is 'champ'?

8. Kimberly and Mikado are famous as what?

9. Who are the 'Saffrons'?

10. Which county might be seen as somewhat depressed?

11. What did an Irish horse lose after winning in Athens in 2004?

12. What were 'the races of Castlebar'?

13. Why was it called 'the races of Castlebar'?

14. Where was Shergar stabled when he was kidnapped in 1983?

15. What was the *Sirius*, and what is its connection to Cork?

16. What is 'dulse'?

17. Which animal was once featured on the reverse of an Irish ten pence coin?

18. What are 'The Waves of Tory'?

19. What was on the menu for Dublin Zoo's lions and tigers during the Easter Rising of 1916?

20. What were the 'Drapier's Letters'?

1. Altamont

2. Camogie

3. The long-extinct Irish Elk

4. Glenariff

5. A Celtic mother goddess

6. Irish tenants in Co. Mayo refused to have anything to do with their landlord's English estate manager, named Boycott

7. An Irish potato dish

8. Jacob's biscuits

9. Antrim's county GAA sides

10. Down

11. A Gold medal. Banned substances were found after tests on the horse 'Waterford Crystal', resulting in disqualification.

12. British retreat from Castlebar to Athlone

13. Some troops covered a distance of 63 miles over a 27-hour period, on foot

14. Ballymany Stud, Newbridge, Co. Kildare

15. The first steam ship to cross the Atlantic, 1838, from Passage West, Co. Cork

16. Dried seaweed

17. Salmon

18. An Irish ceílí dance

19. Supply difficulties meant that some of the other zoo residents became food for the lions and tigers!

20. Anonymous pamphlets critical of England's treatment of Ireland

1. Daniel O'Donnell is a famous Irishman in which sphere?

2. What is the highest point in Co. Wicklow?

3. How long is the Carrick-a-rede rope bridge?

4. Which river valleys converge at the Meeting of the Waters?

5. What is the county town of Armagh?

6. Which county in Connacht is the only one without a coastline?

7. Ireland is roughly the size of which American state?

8. Which Kerry area was once described as 'Heaven's reflex'?

9. What is the importance of Great Saltee, Clare Island and Lambay Island?

10. Near which Armagh church is Brian Boru supposedly buried?

11. What is the name of the English nuclear power station closest to Ireland?

12. Saint Mullins is a historic village on the River Barrow. Name the county.

13. The area of Teltown on the banks of the River Blackwater is in
    which county?

14. Where was Michael Collins imprisoned after the Rising?

15. How high was the dome of Dublin's Custom House?

16. What sort of ancient monument can be found near Clogher, Co. Tyrone?

17. Where is Lough Furnace?

18. St Patrick's Church of Ireland stands on two branches of which Dublin river?

19. From which mountain is the Rock of Cashel supposed to have been formed?

20. Meath, Dublin, Wicklow, Carlow, Laois, Offaly and Westmeath share a
    border with which other county?

1. As a singer

2. Pierce's Table

3. 80 feet

4. Aughrim, Avoca, Gold Mines

5. Armagh

6. Roscommon

7. West Virginia

8. Killarney

9. Ireland's main grey seal breeding ground

10. St Patrick's Church of Ireland

11. Sellafield, in the county of Cumbria

12. Co. Carlow

13. Co. Meath

14. Wales

15. 125 feet

16. Knockmany Passage Grave

17. Co. Mayo

18. Poddle

19. Devil's Bit Mountain, Co. Tipperary

20. Kildare

1. What sport did business magnate Tony O'Reilly once play for Ireland?

2. How many caps did Tony O'Reilly win?

3. How many caps did David O'Leary win with Ireland's football team?

4. Who was the first man to win seven All-Ireland medals?

5. Who became world flyweight boxing champion in 1947?

6. When did Ireland first compete in the Winter Olympics?

7. Who won the World Cup of golf with Paul McGinley in 1997?

8. Which Northern Ireland football manager had a stadium named after him?

9. Which Irish President was once a substitute Irish rugby fullback?

10. Who was the first Ulsterman to head the GAA?

11. Why was 1890's Munster Senior Football final abandoned after 57 minutes?

12. Between which teams was the 1890 Munster Senior Football final contested?

13. Why was the 1899 Cork vs Tipperary match abandoned at half-time?

14. What is unusual about 1900 and 1902 Connacht Senior finals?

15. When was Derry's first All-Ireland Senior Football title?

16. In which sport did Lory Meagher become famous?

17. Eddie Macken represented Ireland at the 1992 and 1996 Olympics in which discipline?

18. Who became IBF world flyweight champion in 1989?

19. When did Stephen Roche win the Tour de France?

20. Which sport do Shelbourne play?

Answers to Quiz 82

1. International Rugby
2. Twenty-nine
3. Sixty-seven
4. 'Danno' O'Keeffe, Kerry goalkeeper
5. Rinty Monaghan
6. 1992
7. Padraig Harrington
8. Danny Blanchflower
9. Éamon de Valera
10. Pádraig MacNamee
11. The football burst
12. Cork and Kerry
13. No ball was available
14. Galway was unopposed in first, in second Galway was awarded the title
15. The 1993 Sam Maguire
16. Hurling
17. Showjumping / equestrian events
18. Dave McAuley
19. 26th July 1985
20. Soccer

1. Where is the town of Mooncoin?

2. In which county is Stillorgan?

3. In which county is the monastic settlement of Clonmacnois?

4. Which city was described as being 'Built on reclaimed mud, hammers playing in the shipyard'?

5. Which counties comprised the Kingdom of Dal Riada?

6. What are the stones in the Lissyviggeen circle also known as?

7. Name the final port of call of the liner *Titanic*?

8. Where did John Redmond die?

9. What was the name of the street in which Wolfe Tone was born?

10. What is the current name of the street where Wolfe Tone was born?

11. Which city is the subject of the ballad 'The Bells of Shandon'?

12. Where was Liam O'Flaherty born?

13. The river Slaney flows through which county?

14. How high are the Cliffs of Moher?

15. In which county is the pilgrimage site of Croagh Patrick?

16. Napper Tandy landed on which Donegal island, on 16th September 1798?

17. Where is The Lios?

18. Where was John Philip Holland born?

19. What was "the shortest route between this country and America"?

20. On which Irish island is there definitely a Mermaid?

1. Co. Kilkenny

2. Co. Dublin

3. Co. Offaly

4. Belfast

5. Antrim in Ireland, Argyllshire in Scotland

6. Seven Sisters

7. Queenstown (Cobh)

8. London, March 1918

9. Stafford Street, No. 44

10. Wolfe Tone Street, Dublin

11. Cork

12. Inishmore island, 1896

13. Carlow

14. 197 metres

15. Co. Mayo

16. Rutland Island

17. Bruff, Limerick

18. Liscannor, Co. Clare

19. Galway–St John's, Newfoundland

20. Ireland's Eye – it is a sea cliff

1. Who wrote the 'Drapier's Letters'?

2. Who is Phildy Hackball?

3. Who traditionally hunted the wren in Ireland?

4. What do *Anacreon* and *Hoche* have in common?

5. The English author of *The Rights of Man* was given honorary membership of which Irish organisation?

6. What special type of bridge spanned Dublin's Royal Canal?

7. A Wild Duck, not a Wild Goose made John Barry a famous sailor. Why?

8. What award did designer Cedric Gibbons receive 'for consistent excellence'?

9. What is Fairyhouse?

10. Which Irish county shares its name with a buoyant wood?

11. What principally connects Killyleagh Co. Down with the British Museum?

12. Why is Rathlin an Irish island, rather than Scottish?

13. What is the origin of Donegal's The Frosses?

14. What is Dublin's North Bull?

15. What are the Paps of Danu?

16. What are pampooties?

17. Which world record was set between Athy, Co. Kildare and Phoenix Park, July 1903?

18. What is the main alcohol ingredient in Irish coffee?

19. What ransom was demanded for the return of Shergar?

20. Of which country is Daniel O'Donnell an 'honorary citizen'?

1. Jonathan Swift

2. A 'fictional author', created by author Patrick McCabe

3. The Wren Boys

4. They were ships involved in the French landings in 1798

5. The United Irishmen

6. Lattice-beam bridge

7. The vessel *Wild Duck* was renamed *Lexington*, captained by Barry

8. The Academy Award

9. A racecourse near Dublin

10. Cork

11. The collection of Sir Hans Sloane

12. A court case in 1617 decided that it must be Irish, for there were no snakes on the island

13. Na Frasa, the showers (possibly of blood)

14. An estuary area, important for wading birds and other wildfowl

15. Mountains in Co. Kerry

16. A type of shoe, once worn on the Aran Islands

17. Land speed record

18. Whiskey

19. £5,000,000

20. Romania (due to his charity work)

1. What is 'keening'?

2. Who would have sung 'Croppies Lie Down'?

3. Who or what was Spring Rice?

4. What is the Tour of the Sperrins?

5. Where is Lord Antrim's Parlour?

6. What hard sweet is Ballycastle's Lammas Fair famous for?

7. Who or what were the Palatines?

8. How long was the bridge across Dublin's Royal Canal?

9. Who was the engineer who designed Dublin's Royal Canal bridge?

10. What was "a wound which Ireland cannot stanch"?

11. When was Brian Friel born?

12. Why could Brian Friel lay claim to two birthdays?

13. How was the Earl of Erne employed from 1855?

14. What was the ILPU?

15. To which O'Brien do we owe the most famous King of the 20th century?

16. What "never came to Ireland until Teilifís Éireann went on the air"?

17. Name the Irish rugby player who won the VC during the Boer War.

18. Which symbol is common to the Irish Euro and pre-decimal coinage?

19. What is another name for an 'executive high ball' in rugby?

20. In which language was Samuel Beckett's poem 'Poem' written?

1. Traditional wailing as a sign of intense grief

2. Orange yeomen in 1798

3. Secretary of State for War and the Colonies in April 1834

4. A motor rally circuit

5. Giant's Causeway

6. Yellowman

7. German Protestant settlers, who came to Ireland in 1709

8. 140 feet

9. Sir John McNeill

10. Queenstown, and the emigration which took place from this port

11. 9th January and 10th January 1928

12. Two birth certificates were issued

13. Irish sea voyages (it was a paddle steamer)

14. Irish Loyal and Patriotic Union, founded in 1885

15. Willis O'Brien, animator of 'King Kong'

16. Sex

17. Thomas Crean

18. The harp

19. Garryowen

20. French

1. Players and staff of which sport are eligible for the Tom Rooney Award?

2. Dave Gallaher was the first captain of which world-beating rugby side?

3. Where did rugby player Dave Gallaher come from?

4. Who played camogie for Dublin across three decades?

5. Paul Russell, a Kerryman, represented which province in 1927?

6. Which province did Paul Russell represent in 1928?

7. What age was Norman Whiteside when he played in his first FA Cup Final?

8. On which island did Paul McGinley and Padraig Harrington win golf's World Cup 1997?

9. Who was the first Irishman to reach the summit of Mount Everest?

10. In what year did Dennis Taylor win snooker's World Championship?

11. In which Olympics did Ireland first compete in the Women's Triathlon event?

12. Which Irish Olympian published a book on the Irish Setter?

13. Who was the first Irishman to win golf's PGA Championship?

14. Which Irishman won a Gold medal in target shooting during the 1908 Olympics?

15. What team played against Ireland in its first soccer international?

16. When did John Watson retire from Formula One?

17. For how many seasons did John Watson compete in Formula One?

18. When was racing driver John Watson born?

19. What was the highest position John Watson achieved in his sport's Championship?

20. Where was motorcycle ace Joey Dunlop born?

1. Rugby – for exceptional contribution to Irish rugby

2. New Zealand's All Blacks

3. Ramelton, Co. Donegal

4. Kathleen Mills (played 1941-61)

5. Munster

6. Leinster

7. Eighteen years, nineteen days old

8. Kiawah Island, South Carolina, USA

9. Dawson Stelfox

10. 1986

11. 2008

12. Joshua Kearney Millner

13. Padraig Harrington, in 2008

14. Joshua Kearney Millner

15. England

16. 1985

17. Twelve

18. 4th May 1946

19. Joint runner-up in the 1982 World Drivers Championship

20. Ballymoney, Co. Antrim

1. When and where was the Orange Order founded?

2. When was New York's first 'St Patrick's Day Parade'?

3. What is taken as the probable date of St Patrick's death?

4. What was notable about Alcock and Brown's landing in Co. Galway?

5. When was the first Irish national lottery held?

6. Where did the Irish Brigade meet Pope Pius XII, 12th June 1944?

7. Which wager is James Daly famous for accepting?

8. Which new word did James Daly popularise, according to 'legend'?

9. What was James Daly's profession?

10. What was the 'Brendan Voyage'?

11. Which famous aviation pairing landed in Co. Galway on 15th June 1919?

12. What were Seventh Heaven and Caveman's Delight?

13. What was opened at Lissadell House in 1925?

14. Which county claims singer Daniel O'Donnell as one of its own?

15. What planet do Zig and Zag come from?

16. Juno (as *Juno and the Paycock*) is the wife of which Roman god?

17. How was Lough Neagh created, according to legend?

18. What is St Patrick said to have done in Black Lough, Gap of Dunloe?

19. How long did the enchantment of the Children of Lir last?

20. What were the names of the Children of Lir?

1. Co. Armagh, 1795

2. 17th March 1762

3. 17th March 461AD

4. They had completed the first transatlantic powered flight

5. 1780

6. In the Vatican

7. The creation of a new, meaningless word, and encourage its common use in twenty-four hours (apocryphal story)

8. Quiz

9. Theatre manager

10. St Brendan is supposed to have discovered America in the 6th century, 900 years before Columbus

11. John Alcock and Arthur Brown

12. Ascents in the Twelve Bens mountains

13. A handball court

14. Donegal

15. Zog

16. Jupiter (although the Captain is not comparable)

17. Finn MacCool scooped up earth; throwing it into the Irish Sea, he unwittingly created the Isle of Man

18. Drowned the last of Ireland's snakes

19. 900 years

20. Aodh, Fionnuala, Conn and Fiachra

1. According to Jacques McCarthy, sports writer, in which sport do you: 'kick the man if you cannot kick the ball'?

2. What was the score in Ireland's first soccer international?

3. According to Jacques McCarthy, sports writer, in which sport do you: 'kick the ball if you cannot kick the man'?

4. In what year did Ireland first win a rugby match at Twickenham?

5. When did motorcycle ace Joey Dunlop die?

6. Which sport do Corinthians play?

7. How many Irish hockey caps did Terry Gregg win?

8. Which sport takes place at Dublin's Harold's Cross Stadium?

9. Which hockey player has captained Ireland, Great Britain and Ulster, winning Olympic Gold and Bronze?

10. What are the Tailteann Games?

11. When were the first 'modern' Tailteann games held?

12. What is the traditional interval between Tailteann games?

13. Which racecourse holds the Irish Champion Stakes?

14. Who was Northern Ireland football manager 2004-2007?

15. Who was Republic of Ireland football manager 1996-2002?

16. Against which side did Tom Arrigan make his sole international appearance in 1937?

17. In which sport was Eddie Irvine a famous participant?

18. Roy Keane was a famous footballer in which three club sides?

19. Tony McCoy is a champion in which sport?

20. Which team won the Senior Hurling championship in 1901?

1. Association (football – soccer)

2. 13-0 in favour of the opposition

3. Gaelic

4. 1929

5. 3rd July 2000

6. Hockey

7. 103

8. Greyhound racing

9. Stephen Martin

10. A modern form of the ancient competitions held between tribes –
    the 'Irish Olympics'

11. 1924

12. Four years

13. Leopardstown

14. Lawrie Sanchez

15. Mick McCarthy

16. Norway

17. Formula One motor-racing

18. Nottingham Forest, Manchester United, Celtic FC

19. National Hunt racing

20. London

1. Where is Barntrosna?

2. What is another name for the Iveagh Peninsula?

3. Where did the Irish Bards meet until 1746?

4. What does the name Ilnacullin mean?

5. Where is The Meeting of the Waters?

6. What is the county town of Tipperary?

7. The village of Tempo is found in which county?

8. There are four Irish counties beginning with 'W'. Name them.

9. What is the longest river in the British Isles?

10. Which county is also a verse form?

11. Near which lake are the Seven Sisters to be found?

12. Where was the *Victorian* – first turbine-engined vessel to cross the Atlantic Ocean – built?

13. Which island is named after an ancient Irish sea-god?

14. 'The Poisoned Glen' is in which county?

15. Where is the HQ of the Army Air Corps?

16. Where did WB Yeats die?

17. Which area is in dispute between Ireland, Great Britain and Norway?

18. In which Irish county is the ancestral home of American President Woodrow Wilson?

19. Which Co. Derry town is named after the feat of a heroic hound?

20. In which county did Hugh O'Neill fight the Battle of Clontibret in 1595?

1. In the books of Patrick McCabe (a fictional Irish town)

2. Waterville Promontory

3. Bruree, Co. Limerick

4. 'Island of holly'

5. Wicklow, near Avoca

6. Clonmel

7. Co. Fermanagh

8. Co. Waterford, Co. Westmeath, Co. Wexford, Co. Wicklow

9. Shannon

10. Limerick

11. Lough Leane

12. Belfast, in 1905

13. Isle of Man, from Manannan

14. Donegal

15. Baldonnel aerodrome, Co. Dublin

16. Cap Martin on the French Riviera

17. Rockall, an outcrop in the Atlantic Ocean

18. Co. Tyrone

19. Limavady ('leim a mhadaidh') leap of the dog

20. Co. Monaghan

1. Name all the Aran Islands.

2. Which part of Co. Meath would be home from home to *felix leo*?

3. Ireland lacks snakes, but it does have a Boa Island. Where is it?

4. In which county is Lough Ahalia?

5. Lugnaquilla is the highest mountain in which county?

6. The Lake of Killarney was once known as?

7. The Blasket Islands lie to the west of which Irish county?

8. Lough Ree has banks along three Irish counties. Name them.

9. In which city did Daniel O'Connell die?

10. Which Cavan town was famous for its spa waters?

11. In which county is Lissyviggeen?

12. Where is Mount Cairnbone?

13. What structure stands on the northern shore of Lake Tacumshane?

14. Which Connemara bay reads as if it might be named after a noted French writer?

15. What was the Lagan Navigation?

16. Where would you find Hare's Castle?

17. What connects the Carrick-a-rede rock with the rest of the island?

18. In which city was the *Messiah* first performed?

19. Which northern Irish town styles itself the 'city of the seven towers', although it possesses no cathedral?

20. In which county are the Caha mountains?

1. Inishmore, Inishmaan, Inisheer

2. Lionsden (*felix leo* is the Latin designation of the lion)

3. Lower Lough Erne in Fermanagh

4. Galway – it's in Connemara

5. Wicklow

6. Lough Lean

7. Co. Kerry

8. Co. Longford, Co. Roscommon, Co. Westmeath

9. Paris, France

10. Swanlinbar

11. Co. Kerry

12. Baillieborough, Co. Meath

13. A windmill, built in 1846

14. Camus

15. An 18th-century canal linking Belfast with Lough Neagh

16. In the Mourne Mountains – it is a climb

17. Rope bridge

18. Dublin

19. Ballymena, Co. Antrim

20. Co. Kerry

1. Lough Gealain lies within which spectacular area?

2. Which is the oldest city in Ireland?

3. Off the coast of which eastern county is Lambay Island?

4. Which saint has an island named after them in Co. Cavan's Templeport Lake?

5. What do the names of the Aran Islands mean in English?

6. Which is the 'metropolitan' county of Ireland?

7. Which body of water may be found near The Lios?

8. Poulaphuca Reservoir in Co. Wicklow is known by what other name?

9. What item of interest may be found on Mount Browne, Co. Carlow?

10. Where were the first 'Irish' Puritans to be found?

11. Where would you be if you thought 'the girls are so pretty'?

12. On which river does Cork stand?

13. Which island off Co. Cork is also known as Ilnacullin?

14. Where is Kiltartan's Cross, the area mentioned in the poem 'An Irish Airman Foresees His Death'?

15. Where is WB Yeats buried?

16. Where were Ireland's last-known prosecuted witches tried?

17. Liscannor, Co. Clare is the site of which particular object of pilgrimage?

18. What is unusual about Mannin Bay in Connemara?

19. Which mountain on Kerry's Dingle peninsula is Ireland's fourth-highest?

20. What is the closest country to the island of Ireland?

1. The Burren

2. Waterford, Co. Waterford

3. Co. Dublin

4. St Mogue

5. Big island, middle island, east island

6. Dublin

7. Lough Gur

8. Blessington Lake

9. A dolmen

10. Lurgan, Co. Armagh, in 1654

11. Dublin's fair city

12. Lee

13. Garinish

14. In Co. Galway, near Thoor Ballylee

15. Drumcliffe churchyard, Co. Sligo

16. Islandmagee, Co. Antrim

17. St Brigid's Well

19. The sand on its shore is made up of fragments of coralline algae, forming 'coral' beaches, rather than the usual silicate sand

19. Brandon Mountain

20. Scotland

1. How many Senators sat in Stormont?

2. What is the important role played by the butterfly in Irish folklore?

3. What was 'gavelkind'?

4. What was Cuchulainn's 'Gae-Bolg'?

5. What were Cuchulainn's horses called?

6. What was Cuchulainn's father-in-law called?

7. Which Irish mythological figure is the equivalent of Gawain's Green Knight?

8. Who or what is Lurigethan?

9. What was the Stranger's challenge to Cuchulainn?

10. Who said "What is the stars"?

11. Which Formula One motor racing team was named after and headed by an Irishman?

12. What did St Brigid famously use to gain land for her religious community?

13. What was unusual about St Brigid's cloak?

14. Which county did Peter Canavan represent in gaelic games?

15. Which Irish aristocrat was Viceroy of India and Governor General of Canada in the 1880s and 1890s?

16. What is another name for the Priory of Lough Derg?

17. How many people made the journey from Belfast to Lisburn by rail on the Ulster Railway's first day in 1836?

18. 'Phelim Brady, the Bard of Armagh' held another office. What was it?

19. What memento of St Patrick did Red Island in Co. Dublin retain?

20. Drumragh and Camowen rivers join to form which other river near Omagh?

1. Twenty-six

2. It is a form taken by a departing soul

3. Distribution of clan land for a fixed number of years

4. A magical spear

5. Grey of Macha, Black of Saingield

6. Forgall the Wily, a druid

7. Uath, the Stranger

8. A hill in the Glens of Antrim

9. That Cuchlainn could behead him only if Uath was allowed to do the same

10. Joxer Daly, from *Juno and the Paycock*

11. Jordan – Eddie Jordan

12. Her cloak

13. It once covered about 12 acres

14. Tyrone

15. 5th Marquis of Lansdowne

16. 'St Patrick's Purgatory'

17. 3000

18. Bishop of Armagh – Terence Donnelly. During the time of the Penal Laws, he ministered in secret.

19. His footprints (carved into the rock where he stood)

20. Strule

1. For which television company did Mary McAleese once work as a journalist and presenter?

2. Which television detective series starred Bond actor Pierce Brosnan?

3. What happens on RTÉ 1 television at 6pm, for one minute?

4. James Ellis starred in which 1960s British police drama?

5. Which character did Colm Meaney play in different *Star Trek* series?

6. Who played *Father Ted*'s housekeeper, Mrs Doyle?

7. What is the family connection between *Ballykissangel* and *Drop the Dead Donkey*?

8. Which actor links *Ballykissangel* and *Drop the Dead Donkey*?

9. Which one-time Director of Britain's Channel Four became President of Ireland?

10. Where is the soap opera *Fair City* set?

11. Who wrote a play based on the tragedy of Ellen Hanley?

12. Who wrote the comic play *The Whiteheaded Boy*?

13. Who wrote the play *The Shadow of a Gunman*?

14. Christy Mahon is the title character in which JM Synge play?

15. Where was Brian Friel born?

16. Which playwright has one of his characters cry 'Take away our hearts of stone and give us hearts of flesh'?

17. Which city features in one of Brian Friel's most famous plays?

18. Which playwright once said "thank you sister, may you be mother to a bishop"?

19. What age was Krapp when he made his 'last tape'?

20. Who wrote the play, *The Informer*?

1. RTÉ

2. *Remington Steele*

3. The Angelus bells ring

4. *Z-Cars*

5. Miles O'Brien

6. Pauline McLynn

7. Tony Doyle (Mr Fitzgerald) is the father of Susannah Doyle (Joy in *Drop the Dead Donkey*)

8. Stephen Thompkinson, as Damien and Father Peter Clifford

9. Mary McAleese

10. Dublin city

11. Dion Boucicault, *The Colleen Bawn*

12. Lennox Robinson

13. Sean O'Casey

14. *Playboy of the Western World*

15. Killyclogher, Co. Tyrone

16. Sean O'Casey

17. Philadelphia, *Philadelphia Here I Come*

18. Brendan Behan

19. Thirty-nine years old

20. Liam O'Flaherty

1. Which internet search engine owes its name to the imagination of Dean Swift?

2. For which fabric is Donegal most famous?

3. Which industrialist made the estate of Glenveagh Castle the marvel it is today?

4. Complete the line 'Low lie the fields of…'?

5. Who buried St Patrick?

6. When is St Brigid's feast day?

7. The pilgrimage site at Knock has an amenity denied many less famous sites. What is it?

8. Which military group met with Pope Pius XII on 12th June 1944?

9. When was Mellifont Abbey founded?

10. Which monastic Order founded Kilcooly Abbey in Tipperary?

11. What was the year of 'Catholic Emancipation'?

12. What is the literal translation of 'Sinn Féin'?

13. What does DUP stand for?

14. Which modern political party developed from Cumann na nGaedheal?

15. In what area of life was Nathaniel Hone notable?

16. Which Dublin-born artist created a 15,000 square feet work of art in an Edinburgh church late in the 19th century?

17. What was the profession of Edward Carson's father?

18. Who wrote 'The groves of Blarney / They look so charming'?

19. Which GAA Army athlete was also an international showjumper?

20. When and where was the Ladies Gaelic Football Association formed?

1. Yahoo, from *Gulliver's Travels*

2. Donegal Tweed

3. Henry McIlhenny

4. 'Athenry'

5. Tassach, a disciple who founded a church in Raholp, Co. Down

6. 1st February

7. An airport

8. The Irish Brigade of the British Army

9. 1142

10. Cistercians

11. 1829

12. 'Ourselves Alone'

13. Democratic Unionist Party

14. Fine Gael

15. He was an Irish artist

16. Phoebe Anna Traquair

17. He was an architect

18. Richard Alfred Milliken, 'The Groves of Blarney'

19. Larry Kiely of Tipperary

20. 1974, Hayes Hotel, Thurles, Tipperary